Playing My Heart Out

Playing My Heart Out

One Ringer's Passion for Handbells

Hillary B. Marotta

Cover Design and typesetting by HR Hegnauer
Editing: Maggie McReynolds, Un-Settling Books
Author's photo courtesy of Jodi Ocker Photography

Advance Praise

In her lovely memoir, Hillary Marotta gives us a fascinating window into an uncommon passion, handbell music. In doing so, she invites her readers to acknowledge, embrace and nurture their own life passions, however uncommon they might be.

—Tim Madigan, author of
I'm Proud of You: My Friendship with Fred Rogers

I read this book start to finish in one night and I was *blown away!* Ms. Marotta nailed this! From the first words to the final pages, I was in the rehearsal room with her, sweating out the auditions, my own self-doubt on full display, heart racing and palms sweaty. Ms. Marotta's description of the internal joy of ringing in concerts had me flying high and falling in love with handbells all over again. I found myself smiling at her descriptions of handbell life that resonated deeply with me. What a gift this is to our handbell community, the musical world at large, and to anyone who wants a peak behind the curtain at what drives passionate musicianship. Every page echoes Ms. Marotta's love of music. Just wow! Stellar job! I will highly recommending this to my ringers!

—Brian Childers, Director of Handbells,
Children and Youth Music, Myers Park UMC,
Author of *Ringing Deeply, Devotions for Bell Ringers*

Playing My Heart Out is a beautiful tribute to pursuing your passions. Ms. Marotta does an excellent job of conveying all that goes into being a handbell musician and the amazing rewards that come from participating in the art form. But this book isn't just for handbell musicians—it's for anyone who wants to follow their passion, whatever it may be. By sharing her journey through one corner of the world of handbells, Ms. Marotta illustrates the importance of being true to your heart and how finding and pursuing your passion leads you to a more complete and fulfilling life.

—Jennifer Cauhorn, Event Consultant, Handbell Musicians of America & Music Director, Queen City Bronze

Table of Contents

*To each person who has brought music
into my life in some way.
You know who you are, and this is for you.
All my love and gratitude.*

Foreword

For a musician, the process of bringing a piece of music to its final stage of development—whether that's practicing for a major performance or learning a new musical concept—is often more important than the moment when everything comes together. That road to the end result, marked by differing amounts of apprehension, joy, stress, elation, and perseverance, can be every bit as fulfilling as the destination.

In this book, Hillary Marotta tells the story of her journey on that road and of opening her heart to what has become a major part of her life: the world of handbells and handbell ringing. It's a story of passion and discovery, of how handbells led her down an amazing musical path she never would have believed possible. As an accomplished ringer and handbell conductor, Hillary has learned that at the center of every rehearsal and performance is our very soul, our passion. Hillary's book gives us unique access into her initial self-doubts and her final triumphant acknowledgement that everyone can follow their instincts when it comes to pursuing those things they love most.

I am honored to be a part of Hillary's story. From the perspective of teacher to student, and now as close friend and colleague, I have witnessed the awesome and exciting transformation from a woman who wished to be a musician to a confident and knowledgeable communicator and leader in the field. Hillary guides us from her early training as a pianist, flutist, and high school drum major through many hills and valleys as she continually questioned and measured her own justification for moving forward with her passion. Hillary reveals, in a very honest and sincere approach, the many stages one must pass through in the journey of finding our place, that place in the heart that tells us, "You must do this!"

One of my great passions (besides my family and my music) is back-packing in the wilderness. Hillary's journey can be likened to a challenging hike—difficult but also very rewarding as one forges ahead, reaches a destination, and realizes how worthwhile it was to make the trip.

You will read of Hillary's struggles with self-worth when confronted with the unknown. But her honest and sincere desire to follow her passion kept her on track, one step at a time, to create incredible music collectively as a ringer, and interpretively as a conductor who has the huge responsibility of becoming the interpreter of a composer's soul. I shall never forget the look on Hillary's face the first time she conducted in front of an audience. With tears streaming down my face, I saw relief, yes, but also her calming sense of accomplishment, knowing all of her inner struggles to get to that point in her life.

Finally, I am humbled and flattered that there is way too much of this book about me ... but as I comprehend all that she shares in this book, I realize we are all in this together. Through all of her experiences, including extreme emotional highs and lows, Hillary makes it clear in this book that we are all reflections of sincere and honest emotion and reaction.

When she was my student at Bucknell University, Hillary was always dedicated to the aesthetic experience, always, always open to new horizons that touch the heart. Because of this, Hillary learned to be unafraid to open to those who need to experience this same passion. I applaud her courage and conviction.

—William A. Payn

Introduction

One sunny October Sunday in 1997, I went to the interdenominational chapel service at my new home, Bucknell University. It was my freshman year, and I was floundering emotionally. In fact, I was the most homesick I'd ever been, the kind of homesick that made me gag on my toothbrush every morning and call home sobbing every night. I even lost the freshman fifteen everyone else was gaining.

Church felt like a way to maintain some kind of normalcy. Attendance had been mandatory when I was growing up, but now I actively wanted to be there. I was motivated by faith, sure, but also by the fact that the entire enterprise, from getting ready to finishing lunch afterward, took up at least three hours of my otherwise empty day.

The university's Rooke Chapel was gorgeous, a serene, unbroken white canvas save for the wood finishing on the ends of the pews. The cathedral ceiling was vast, amplifying the congregation's music and other sounds instead of echoing emptily. I liked the expansiveness of it. It looked nothing like my home church, and I was surrounded by strangers—but I was comforted there.

At one point during the service, the Rooke Chapel Ringers, Bucknell's handbell choir, got up to play in the open space near the altar. I took a deep breath and exhaled with disinterest. I'd had a run-in with handbells before, and it hadn't gone well. This, I thought, was something I'd have to grit my teeth and get through.

Then the first notes hit me like lightning. I sat up straight, a cartoon word balloon spelling "Aha!" practically materializing over my head. The hair stood up on my arms, and I shivered. In the music that came from those bells, I heard blended harmonies and countermelodies. I heard a clear rhythm and moments of smooth nuances in dynamics. The soft melody gently grew into fuller phrases, culminating in a rich, round sound that enveloped the beautiful chapel and everyone in it. I don't think I took a single breath during the entire piece.

When it was over, I had to consciously close my mouth, unaware until then that it had been hanging open in amazement. I didn't know it yet, but I'd just experienced more than a simple change of heart about handbells. This moment, as it turned out, would alter the trajectory of my life.

Like most people, I've played many roles in my life—ones I chose and ones I felt forced into. I've had jobs and responsibilities and seemingly endless lists of to-dos, like doing the dishes or keeping the house clean (or figuring out a new normal in a pandemic). We're all doing some kind of juggling act.

We also have these great brains and big hearts that give us the capacity to think and feel, to find the motivation, enthusiasm, and passion for something that gets us through the everyday. These are the things that light us up from the inside, that make our hearts race and our tummies flip-flop. These are the things that bring us happiness and fulfillment beyond the requisite roles we play in our lives. These are the things that give us the feeling of being fully alive. Our passions may all be different, but the love we have for them is a common, shared experience.

I have passion for many things in my life, including but not limited to helping and educating others, working in the nonprofit industry, and being a mental health advocate. I get paid for some of them, but not most. It's a select few of us who get paid to do exactly what lights up our souls. Sometimes I think it's too bad more people can't make money doing the things they love, but then again, I wonder if that compensation would make our passions lose their luster and become more mundane? Is it possible that not getting paid to do what we love makes us love it all the more?

What I love is music. Music is the companion who never abandons me. It lifts me up when I'm down and brings me to tears of joy, release, and gratitude. It connects my heart to other hearts in ways that words can't. It makes my soul come alive, and gives me comfort. Music is what I always return to; it's my home.

I love music of all kinds, but my passion is handbells. I find them fascinating, beautiful, and utterly unique. They've been likened to keyboards, percussion instruments, and even vocalists because they have commonalities with all three, and yet they have an expression all their own, from their sound to the way they're played.

I had no idea what handbells could do until that moment in the Rooke Chapel. But once I heard them played at a level I'd never experienced before, I was hooked. I knew I had to make them part of my life, and I have ever since. My passion for handbells has given me unending joy, precious friendships, and lessons that apply in all areas of my life.

Our passions, no matter what they are, are like that: wonderful growth opportunities that open our minds and our hearts. Whether you share my enthusiasm for handbells or feel fulfilled by sewing or cooking or running or reading, we can all relate to each other in the ways that our passions ignite us.

1

The Discovery
of What Moves Us

Music gives a soul to the universe,
wings to the mind, flight to the imagination,
and life to everything.
—Plato

Bucknell felt like the first time I'd ever heard handbells—but it wasn't.

When I was around eleven, our church started a handbell choir. At the time, I had no idea what handbells even were. I'd never even heard them played.

I didn't know (and, likely, didn't care) about the history of handbells. I didn't know they were custom-cast from bronze and finely hand-tuned. I didn't know that while they'd started out centuries ago in European churches, they'd since gone global and even somewhat mainstream, with ringers playing anything from classical to rock and pop. All I knew was that they seemed pretty dumb, and the choir seemed like just another way for my parents to keep me busy and accounted for. Like church attendance, choir participation wasn't optional. I was simply told I'd be joining, and that was that.

Even though I didn't want to be there, I had a group of friends who'd also joined up, and that made it bearable. We'd pretty much grown up together in the church, singing in the children's choir, attending Sunday school, and going to youth group. We had a lot of fun, especially when we got into giggle fits typical of middle school girls. We especially loved to tell very stupid jokes whose origins I never knew. One of them practically brought us to our knees in laughter whenever one of us told it: "There were three pigs in a bathtub. One pig said to the other pig, 'Pass me the soap.' The other pig said, 'What do you take me for, a typewriter?'" Unsurprisingly, we were often shushed by our director, Mrs. Sibole, because we weren't paying enough attention.

Mrs. Sibole was tough. On the outside, she was a middle-aged mom with a sweet smile and generally pleasant demeanor. Inside, she was a perfectionist—at least when it came to bells. She was relentless about getting us to play the right notes, in the right way, while not talking during rehearsal—an almost impossible combination for a bunch of tween girls. She was particularly militant about two things: our form and making sure we didn't clank any bells together, the latter an abominable sin rectified only by paying a penance of a quarter to a rapidly filling jar. She despaired of our arm movements. "Do not scoop!" she would cry. "You are not digging a garden with your bell!"

Of course it wasn't all bad. She had moments of empathy that endeared her to us, particularly when she sought our input on what we wanted to be named and what we wanted to wear. We became the Rainbow Ringers, dressed in black on the bottom and different color mock turtlenecks on top.

But then it came time to actually play our songs in church, and that's when things went downhill fast. I was terrified to get up there. While handbells are intended to be played as a group, each ringer has two specific notes that she alone is responsible for. No one else in the entire choir is covering those two notes. If she misses a note, or plays a wrong one, no one else can fix it. There's either an odd silence, or, God forbid, a discordant note played not only loudly but also completely (and obviously) wrong.

On this particular Sunday, we began playing our fairly easy piece, and mistakes immediately abounded. Wrong notes here, missing notes there. It appeared as though the choir was operating in several different tempos and time signatures. It was a classic musical train wreck. A really good director of really good musicians can often avoid that wreck at the last second, and the audience is none the worse for the wear. This was not the case here.

"Stop!" Mrs. Sibole ground us to a halt right in the middle of our song. We were shocked that she'd interrupted us, no matter how off we were, and we were flustered and ashamed. I was so embarrassed that my cheeks burned and my throat tightened as if I was going to cry. I don't remember what she said, if anything, or whether she addressed the congregation. The whole experience remains a blur of humiliation.

We began again and ended up finishing our song, but even though the congregation was kind and gracious to us, the damage to our egos, not to mention our enthusiasm for handbells, was done. I wanted to quit immediately, but my parents were having none of that. My friends and I trudged along, but sure as you're reading this, I walked out of there at the end of the year and never looked back. I swore off handbells for the rest of my life, as did several of the other girls. Buh-bye. Fortunately, this didn't sour my love of music. I went on to play flute in marching band in high school, and I loved it.

Some of my friends from the handbell choir came along too, and we happily became marching band geeks—our conversations from August through November centered on what we were playing, where we were competing, and how we did. The season was particularly rough for one friend who was not in marching band and had to endure lunch with us every day. As with most things I loved, I went all in.

Marching band significantly raised my musical game. We were each assigned a number corresponding to a dot on pages and pages of grid maps of the football field. We learned how to march from dot to dot, no easy feat in and of itself, all while moving our feet with a very particular heel-to-toe roll so each step was smooth and uniform. Marching with our feet going one way while our upper bodies remained parallel to the sidelines of the football field was challenging enough, but we'd also have to play our memorized songs with all the musical nuance we could muster.

It truly was an amazing thing, almost like a full-time job in addition to school. Starting in the blazing heat of mid-August, we spent almost a week of nine-hour days playing and marching. Those rehearsals entailed long afternoons of standing in the middle of a football field under the hot sun, our cheeks flushed and sweat dripping everywhere. There was no shade for breaks, and it was both mentally and physically exhausting. Football games were Friday nights, and marching band competitions were all over our region Saturday nights into very early Sunday mornings. And the season was long—from those muggy days of August through mid-November, when we would inevitably have at least one game or competition in the cold, raw rain or even a snow flurry.

Eventually, excitingly, I became one of the band's two drum majors, and got to serve in that role for two years. I led the band on the field and conducted the music from a raised platform so everyone could see me—and so the other drum major and I could keep them together from one 30-yard line to the other. I loved the physicality of it. I also loved being in charge, being a role model, and being responsible for the group, knowing they relied on me to stay together and keep time. It was a thrill and an ego boost—embarrassing to admit, but not uncommon among drum majors—to stand on the podium and accept awards on the band's behalf.

It was also not without challenges. One weekend, we had an away football game on Friday evening and the biggest competition of the season scheduled for the next night. That Friday, I started getting a cold. Nothing terrible, I thought, but during our halftime show, I blanked out on the podium for the first time (and thankfully the last time) ever. For at least eight to twelve counts, I had no idea where we were in the music, what I was supposed to be doing, what pattern I was supposed to be beating, and even what song we were playing. I could feel myself starting to panic—were my cheeks getting red? Was it becoming alarmingly apparent to the audience that I was clueless? Luckily, my conducting partner got me back on track.

Over that night and into next morning, my cold got much worse, and I ended up losing my voice completely. This didn't bode well for the competition that night, which was the last of the year and would determine whether we continued on to the Atlantic Coast Championships, the grand finale of the season.

I "talked" it over with my co-drum major and the band director, and we figured out how we were going to get around me being voiceless. The drum major on the podium usually counts off the beats out loud, supplemented by clapping, in order to tell the band when to move and play. Instead, my partner stood close to the podium and loudly counted off the beats while I clapped, and then she hurried to the spot where she would then conduct her own section of the band.

The crowd probably never noticed, but the judges of the competition, some of whom were on the field with the band as it performed, were very confused. They expected the voice to come from me and, when it didn't, they did double-takes. We found it hilarious, like we were playing a joke on them. It was one of very few things that got me through as I kept getting sicker and sicker on that damp, cold November evening. We didn't end up scoring high enough to go on to the championships, but I think we did the best we could under the circumstances. Not just any band could handle performing with a silent conductor.

Marching band taught me commitment and dedication. It pushed me and grew me through its lessons about hard work, persistence, and leadership. It led me to the good and comforting sense of community and camaraderie musicians create among themselves. As a high schooler, it was reassuring to know that whatever happened in other social circles, we always had our marching band friends. And as I grew in age and musicianship, that sense of connection and belonging would become more and more important.

There was no marching band at Bucknell University, so I played flute in the symphonic band for four years. This was where I learned to really play music well. It was also where I realized that musicians come to rehearsal with their parts already learned! Instead of learning our pieces at rehearsal, we were instead focused on putting the music together, ironing out the intricacies so that the individual players would become one musical group. My college director, Dr. William Kenny, pushed me harder than I'd ever been pushed musically before. And sitting next to high-level musicians was motivating and encouraging.

It was then that I began to realize that music could be as emotionally intricate and moving as things in the tangible world. It was nothing less than life-changing to learn to breathe together, get soft and loud together, and really bring out the delicate parts of the music as a group. We were working as one to evoke a reaction from the audience, to take them on a journey, to make them feel the emotion in the music. Dr. Kenny was brilliant in his ability to explain and describe what he wanted from us as musicians. The nuances we learned to play began to evoke emotions in me, reminding me of people and places and things. Music, whether I was playing it or listening to it, could make me happy, sad, angry, even nostalgic.

We began to create real beauty and refinement in our music, with soft moments, heart-racing moments, and moments of subtlety so sweet that it had our audiences on the edges of their chairs. We formed connections between ourselves and Dr. Kenny and knew by just a glance from him how well we had done. Though it was a rare occasion, we even got the incredulous teary eye from him now and again. In those moments, we knew we had really hit the right nerve and note. I grew exponentially as a musician in college. So much more was expected of me, and all of it was rewarding.

I met Fred, the man who would become my husband, in the symphonic band at Bucknell, and music has continued to wind its way throughout our life. There's always a song in my head—we listen to music in the car, over dinner, at night when going to sleep, in movies. Fred and I joke that while our kids may not get any athletic ability, we hope they'll inherit some musical ability from at least one of us. Maybe flute or handbells from me; maybe clarinet or saxophone from him.

We even gave our daughters names from the music we love. Our oldest, Ella, is named for Ella Fitzgerald, and our younger daughter, Laina, is named after a Billy Joel song called "All for Leyna." Both girls had beginner instruments and went to music class as toddlers. Now Ella plays ukulele and sings, and Laina has memorized lyrics and singers like no other eight-year-old we know. Exposing them to as much music as we can, helping them nurture a love for music in all forms, is important to both of us.

I want my daughters to learn what I have: that music touches people in ways other things can't. As a culture, we use music where words can't quite explain what we want to say or how we want to say it. We use music to enhance and add effect, to convey what we just can't articulate. Imagine removing soundtracks from movies—what would it feel like?

Music is innate in all of us. Humans have made sounds as long as we've been a species, and music, even in its most basic forms, has been used to communicate, to heal, to celebrate, and to mourn. Objects have been beaten like drums since the dawn of time. As humans found their ability to make sounds, voices have sung, wailed, and comforted. Music pumps us up, calms us down, and inspires us. Music takes us other places.

Most of my emotional memories are tied to music in some way. I fell in love with my first boyfriend when he wrote a piano song for me as a Christmas gift in 1995. I'll never get rid of that cassette tape. It still puts an incredulous smile on my face to think that someone wrote me a song. My second boyfriend introduced me to Dave Matthews, for which I remain truly grateful. In fact, we just pulled some Dave Matthews out the other day, and everything came rushing back. I told my husband I need to listen to more Dave because it makes me feel good.

Our high school slide show was set to U2, so each time I hear "Where the Streets Have No Name," it brings back the day of my high school graduation, the memories of walking through our halls with people I had spent every weekday with for twelve years, knowing that only those 169 of us have that particular connection. More recently, I find myself re-watching the video of my courageous Ella in fourth grade in which she, with very few formal lessons, belted out "Count on Me" by Bruno Mars while playing it on her ukulele in front of the entire class. What a full heart, beaming with pride and moved to tears, that memory produces.

Without music, my life would be gray and colorless, boring and mundane, with no magic whatsoever. Music gives my life meaning and connection. It's my passion, the thing that gives me life, something even Plato knew the power of when he said, "Music gives a soul to the universe, wings to the mind, flight to the imagination, and life to everything."

2

Falling in Love with Something Cool

*Life seems to go on without effort
when I am filled with music.*
—George Eliot

I fell in love with handbells that moment in the Rooke Chapel, and I knew I had to find a way to become a part of this group. I wanted to be up there ringing and making that beautiful music with them. But since the semester had already begun, that year's handbell choir had been solidified, already practicing and performing. Disappointingly, I had to wait until the following academic year to even try out.

When sophomore year arrived, though, I was ready. I'd come back to campus early to train to be a Resident Assistant, and that meant I had the chance to get into the music building before anyone else and sign up for one of the coveted handbell choir audition spots, which always filled quickly. I had no idea how many ringers he needed to complete that year's choir.

With great anticipation, I wrote my name on the audition sheet taped to the conductor's office door. (It was 1998, after all.)

At the time, Bucknell's music building was something of a death trap, the equivalent of a starving artist's garret but at a wealthy liberal arts college. It was built over a stream that frequently flooded—I'm not sure what genius engineered that feat—so the ugly, green-carpeted practice rooms in the basement were crawling with black mold and mildew. There was barely any sound proofing, and the building was literally falling apart: paint peeling, ceiling tiles coming down, floorboards decaying. If it were still standing that way today, it's hard to imagine any musician choosing to attend Bucknell, but it's not. The school built a gorgeous, state-of-the-art music and performance building before I left campus in 2001, and it has everything a college music department needs, including a beautiful auditorium.

Auditions took place at the chapel, which is where the choir rehearsed and where the bells lived. Bells take up a lot of room both to play and to store. They come in ascending sizes weighing from just a few ounces to ten to fifteen pounds, and even the smallest ones require hard-shell cases (usually black) lined in both formed foam and soft (usually red) velvet to protect them. Smaller bells get stored several to a case, but big ones can only fit in one. It's a lot of cases.

Once unloaded from their cases, handbells need a lot of floor space. Setting them up means lining up three- and six-foot tables topped with foam pads, tablecloths, and then, finally, the bells. Between the cases, the foldable tables, and all of the other equipment (sheet music, music stands, and other miscellaneous accoutrements), that's a significant chunk of real estate.

Bucknell's handbells had been purchased for the Rooke Chapel Ringers by the philanthropic Robert Rooke, whose parents Charles M. and Olive S. Rooke, had been Bucknell alumnae who loved the school and music, and for whom the chapel was named. The bells were well-loved and used in chapel services as well as multiple Christmas Candlelight Services and a spring concert.

The night of my audition, there were only a few bells on one table. By my sophomore year, I felt more confident in myself as a student and community member, but this was new territory. There were a bunch of upperclassmen there, some I recognized and some I didn't, though no one I actually knew. I expected to see the previous year's conductor there as well, but he was nowhere to be found.

There was, however, a man I'd never seen before. He was tall and skinny, his long, white hair pulled back in a ponytail and somewhat balding on top. With a button-down shirt, tie, and dress pants, he very much looked the part of professor at the university, but his long hair added the mystique of an artist. The students seemed to enjoy a casual, friendly rapport with him, laughing and joking, but at the same time, he was clearly revered. The students moved quickly and adeptly, anticipating his requests, following his lead, and doing whatever he asked. They also hung on his every word, like they knew he could impart a nugget of wisdom at any moment.

I could see that they looked up to him both as a musician and a professor. I could tell from how eagerly they seemed to want to please him that he was someone they wanted to do well for, that him being disappointed in them would be a terrible fate. Yet even he didn't seem to know how adored he was. He had no air of arrogance or self-importance even though, as I later found out, he had every right to.

The reason I'd never seen this man before was because he'd been on sabbatical during my freshman year. The conductor I'd seen that year had been a substitute. Even I could see that this man was on a different level musically, professionally, and in his relationship to the students than his substitute. I immediately felt something special between him and the choir.

It was a huge blessing that I had no idea who he was or how renowned he was in the bell world, or I would have never signed up in the first place. It turned out I was auditioning for Dr. Willian Payn and his Rooke Chapel Ringers, one of the best college handbell choirs in the entire country. I didn't know it yet, but I would learn that Dr. Payn was and is one of the most well-known, respected, and sought-after conductors and composers in the handbell world, although to all of his students and ringers at Bucknell, he was simply and affectionately known as DP.

Once I got to know DP, I got more curious about the details of his career, which he was more than willing to share. He'd graduated from the distinguished Westminster Choir College, and had his first experience with handbells at age 24, when he became the music director for the Second Presbyterian Church in Newark, New Jersey, and conducted a high school choir of female ringers. The church had a five-octave set of Whitechapel Bells made in Tower Hamlets, England, and he became so intrigued by them that he began to search for opportunities for the choir to perform outside of church services.

One day, chuckling at himself, he told me the story of taking the choir to a bell festival for the first time. He recalled, "It was so embarrassing. I had taught the kids to ring the bells, but I had such little experience that I didn't know that most ringers stop the sound. All of my ringers just played continuous notes without damping their bells. I didn't even know what damping was. Luckily, everyone at that festival was very gracious to me and the kids."

All along, his choir had been ringing the bells and letting them vibrate every note, making them sound like a piano with the sustain pedal continually held down. While that sound is lovely and often used in handbell music, it's not the default way to play. Unless it's otherwise marked in the music, everyone damps or stops the sound of their ringing bell, usually against their shoulder or on a padded table.

DP was chagrinned that he didn't know this simple skill. Everyone else at the festival, however, was amazed that his group owned five octaves of bells—most choirs of the day had only two to four. He and his choir took such great lessons away from that first festival that he became even more enamored of the instrument, so much so that he began to compose for it as well.

After a couple years, his career took him to the Presbyterian Church on the Green in Morristown, New Jersey, where he served as the director of music, highlighting his significant skill as an organist. I have wonderful memories of listening as DP, all his students gathered around him and the organ in the chapel, played Widor's "Toccata." The six-minute piece is best known as recessional music and has a level of difficulty organists spend years trying to master. DP was famous around campus for it, and the students looked forward to that moment at the end of Christmas Candlelight Services when he'd play it every year. It was a glorious celebration of our semester being over, Christmas coming, and our hard work paying off.

Watching DP's hands and feet busily create such a masterpiece became a staple of my college experience, so much so that when Fred and I got married, we asked him to play it. There were many beautiful and meaningful moments in that ceremony, but for me, there was nothing more special than DP being a part of our wedding that day in that way, tying together not only my musical experience with him but also the fact that my husband and I were tied together through Bucknell.

While in New Jersey, DP started a handbell program incorporating several youth choirs. That was in the early 1970s, when churches were hubs of the community and many youth activities. The Church on the Green had three octaves of bells, but American bell companies had begun to make two additional octaves. And once you become a bell enthusiast, you want all of the bells. The young choir was so determined to get those two extra octaves that they went for a Guinness Book of World Records record in non-stop handbell ringing as a fundraiser. They rang for over twenty-four hours straight, allowed to break only for meals and to sub in other ringers when someone needed a potty break or a nap.

And they broke the record! After what must have been an exhausting feat even for teens with youthful energy, they raised the money and earned themselves two brand new octaves of Schulmerich bells. What a level of dedication, especially for teenagers, to be on their feet, legs aching, notes most likely swimming on the pages by the end, for 24 hours to get something they really wanted as a group. I would come to see that for DP, this was simply another example of how far his students would go for him and the art of handbells.

After DP went through graduate school at West Virginia University, an additional church job, and eventually a doctorate degree, an opening came up at Bucknell for a position that combined university organist, Chapel Choir director, and adjunct faculty for the music department. Known by this time for his work with handbell choirs, he told administrators during his interview, "If I'm chosen for the position, I will require handbells and a handbell choir." He was quickly offered the position, and the Rooke family purchased a three-octave set of Malmark handbells for the chapel. Within a year, DP became a full-time faculty member.

DP's new handbell choir, the Rooke Chapel Ringers, took off right away, in no small part because some of the students he'd taught in Morristown became students at Bucknell, helping to recruit others and promote this cool new-to-Bucknell instrument. DP felt confident that handbells would be popular at a school like Bucknell because the population there was similar to the one he'd served in Morristown—many high achievers who were dedicated and very committed. And that's what happened. The choir flourished from 1983 to 2014 under his tenure, and although I didn't know it, by the time I got to college in 1997, there were kids who'd been planning to go to Bucknell because of DP and his handbell choir.

His choral groups did well too. His Rooke Chapel Choir repeatedly took my breath away when they performed in chapel services on Sundays. I knew that unless I planned to worship in the future at a professional music school, there would be no other Sunday morning experience like it after Bucknell. DP was able to take his renowned choirs to sing in places like the Ely and Coventry Cathedrals in the United Kingdom and the Salzburg Cathedral in Austria.

DP became a master conductor and composer, serving as conductor and clinician (think teacher, professor, or master) for vocal and bell festivals all over the world. When DP retired, Bucknell honored him with the establishment of the William

A. Payn Scholarship, an endowment fund that annually provides tuition for one deserving incoming music student. Since retirement from Bucknell, DP has continued his over twenty years of service as the Music Director and Conductor of the Susquehanna Valley Chorale, something he enjoys and looks forward to each season.

If I'd known any of this, I really might have turned around and run out the door.

I had no idea what to expect of the audition process, but I was nervous as hell. Although I suffer from generalized anxiety, I was surprised by how jittery I was over this audition. I knew I wanted a spot in this choir, but until I walked into the chapel that night, I hadn't felt in my gut how much. It had been such a long time since I wanted something this badly! My belly was doing somersaults, my jaw was clenched, and my fingernails were digging into my palms, even though I tried to look cool and calm.

Also, my hands were shaky and sweaty—not a good combination for handbells. This played into one of my greatest fears about that audition: I didn't have any gloves. In my only previous experience with bells, Mrs. Sibole had drilled the dire need for gloves into our preteen heads. She always reminded us how extremely delicate and expensive the bells were. If we didn't treat them correctly, she warned us, we wouldn't be able to play.

I later learned from DP that this was only partially true. Originally, ringers wore gloves to protect the leather handles of the bells from the oils on their hands. But most bells in current use have plastic handles, making gloves unnecessary. A related misunderstanding is that ringers wear gloves to protect the bronze part of the bell, but that's also not quite true. Although the oils on our hands can make those beautiful bronze castings dirty, they don't actually harm the bell. The bells simply need more frequent cleaning and polishing to look nice. Many church, school, and community groups that have only one bell choir or one set of people using the bells ring without gloves. In instances where many different people are using the bells many times a week, conductors often make gloves mandatory, but only to cut down on cleaning and polishing.

No one appeared to notice or care whether I was wearing gloves, so I hoped for the best as I picked up two bells and listened to what I was asked to do. I had to do a few simple exercises, read some music, and show how I could manipulate multiple bells in quick succession. All in all, it was a very simple audition. Dr. Payn (not yet DP to me at that time) asked me some questions about my experience with handbells, my overall musical experience, and my involvement with activities at Bucknell.

I knew that in the coming hours or days he would most likely check with some references inside and outside the music department for the full scoop on this management and Spanish double major. I worried that my auditioning in my sophomore rather than my freshman year might work against me. Would I be able to break into this group now? Time would tell because in less than fifteen minutes, my audition was over.

Thankfully, I only had to wait a couple of days before I found out: I had been accepted into the Rooke Chapel Ringers (RCR). I was thrilled! Of course, this turn of events came as a surprise to most of the people in my life including me, because of, well, swearing off bells and all.

It had been at least seven years since I'd touched a bell, save for my audition. Although I'd had that church experience, I knew more would be expected of me and these bells than ever before, and that made me a little apprehensive. I hardly had any experience. I might totally suck. I might not be able to keep up. Maybe I was just an imposter, having only played for one year. What if I got kicked out?

Social anxiety also kicked in. What if they didn't like me? What if they thought I was the nerdiest person they'd ever met? What if I just didn't fit in? And I was still stressing about the glove situation. Were we to wear gloves, were we not, how would I get a pair?

Looking back, I'm so happy that none of those things kept me from trying something new. I would have missed out on what became a pivotal part of my college career, not just musically, but academically and socially. There would have been such a richness missing from my college experience, not to mention the great memories that only DP and the RCR could have given me.

Those first few rehearsals went by in a blur. I was having fun, awakening to what bells could be and do. It was nothing like what I'd done in middle school. We also didn't rehearse like we did in middle school. Even though we got a half-credit in music for playing, we didn't have a rehearsal time scheduled by the university. We all simply checked our schedules (again, paper schedules, back then), and decided when we were available to rehearse.

It turned out the only time everyone could get together was 9:30–11:00 on Thursday nights. It might not have seemed crazy to most college kids, but I was an anomaly. I went to bed every night at 11, and if I was out any longer, my friends and hallmates teased me incessantly about missing my bedtime.

DP, it turned out, shared my opinion. He was not fond of those late-night rehearsals. They made his day extremely long, and he would end up going home for dinner, getting comfy in his chair by the fire, and then having to untangle himself from his blanket and his dog to return to campus. Plus he couldn't have his wine with dinner. At late-night rehearsals, I often heard him say, "I should be in my jammies." Me too, man.

Looking back now, it seems even more like a horrible time to rehearse. I mean, now my bedtime is even earlier. How did I ever do that? Maybe it was the fact that I was so young at the time. Or maybe it was about how dedicated I was and how passionately I cared about bells. When we love something that lights us up, we make room for it whenever and wherever we can. Passion doesn't punch a clock.

The first two bells I played with the ensemble were B4 and C5. Bells mimic a piano keyboard, with one handbell playing the note of one key. In theory, that would mean we'd need eighty-eight handbells to play every key on a piano, but bells can't be made that low because of the gigantic sizes that would be necessary to get those bass notes. That's why bells only come in seven octaves—and owning all seven is wildly expensive. At that time, Bucknell had six.

B4 and C5 were notated by middle C on the piano and the B below it, with the accompanying sharps and flats for each note, even though handbells sound an octave higher than they are written. That meant I had four bells, total, though I shared two of them with my neighbors. On my left, I shared B Flat with my male neighbor, a freshman. On my right, I shared C Sharp with my neighbor Shelly, a fellow sophomore. She would have needed to play that bell any time there was a D Flat.

This was Shelly's second year with the RCR, so she knew the ropes and procedures. She also had a casual style I admired. Her ringing was relaxed, and it looked like it flowed effortlessly.

Nothing seemed to fluster her, and she was a master at watching DP and "getting her head out of the music," as we call it. She was always calm and helpful to me. I'm still envious of the ease with which she turned pages with bells still in her hand, a skill I am working on mastering.

I was also mesmerized by the girls who played the small, high bells and needed to hold at least two bells in each hand rather than one. That requires a lot of dexterity, especially since each bell has to be rung in a different direction. For one note, the bell must be rung as it normally would. For the other note, you ring it like you're knocking on a door to get the clapper to move. Managing four or six different notes in potentially different rhythms necessitates great skill. The way they could maneuver all those bells and play the right notes made my jaw drop. I wanted to be up playing those bells one day.

As the semester wore on, I learned the logistics for ringing in chapel services, how much dedication and commitment was required to be a part of the group, and what our most important performances of the year demanded from us. Equally important, I learned how to practice ringing bells without having actual bells to practice on. That certainly required some creativity, since we weren't allowed to take the bells home to practice. They were expensive and difficult to haul, and in any event most of us lived in dorms and houses where practicing would not be socially accepted or appreciated. And there was much too much risk of damaging or losing a bell. Instead, many of us took our music home each week, sat on our beds, and laid out pens, highlighters, or spoons in the arrangement of our bells. We could sing the music aloud or in our heads and follow our parts as they came up. Even now, I can do this silently without disturbing anyone.

This is still how most people practice, unless they're lucky enough to have their own set of bells, which is rare. Although it's not ideal, it's the best way to ingrain the music in our heads and develop the muscle memory that takes over after we play a piece so many times. And our pieces required a lot of practicing, not only to get the notes down but to show dedication and commitment to the group. When someone came to a rehearsal not knowing his or her part, it took time away from the group actually making music and progress together. We practiced as much for ourselves as for the good of the group. We really wanted to be good musicians.

Our most important performances of each fall semester were our Christmas Candlelight Services. A long-standing tradition developed by DP in the 1980s, Candlelight Services at Rooke Chapel were a masterful combination of Nativity lessons and carols that the Rooke Chapel Choir, the Rooke Chapel Ringers, and various individual musicians played. The chapel was splendidly decorated with a huge Christmas tree lit by hundreds of warm, white sparkling lights, fresh green wreaths, and yards and yards of garland. The air of the great space was filled with the scent of fresh fir. Taped once every four years by the local PBS station, *A Bucknell Candlelight Christmas* was an Emmy-nominated special that signaled the true beginning of the season at the school.

Those Candlelight Services will always be a part of the way I experience Christmas. They were incredibly moving, and they were able to distract me from the hustle and bustle we've made of the holiday season and allow me to focus on the story of the Nativity. The Bible readings were a huge part of that, but so was the music.

We prepared eight to ten pieces of music for those services, from slow and thoughtful traditional carols to quick-paced and celebratory original arrangements. We always finished our set with Kevin McChesney's "Festive Dance," a transcription of George Bizet's "Farandole." The piece is an upbeat version of the original, both challenging and fun to play. Over the years, it became the Rooke Chapel Ringers' signature piece, mostly because we loved to play it. We carried it over from Candlelight Services into tour and spring performances because it was always a fan favorite.

The most fun part of it is the fast-paced malleting (tapping the bells with a rubber-headed mallet) of most of the bells. Every Rooke Chapel Ringer group has tried to go faster and faster to blow the previous choir out of the water. It closes all of the concerts and is usually played a second time as an encore, and all bets are off the table then as to how fast the low bells, who start the malleting, will take it. It brings such a smile to my face just thinking about us ringing that piece, going faster and faster until there was no need for DP to even conduct.

Although he couldn't pull it off during the ceremonious Candlelight Services, we came to expect that DP would mess with us at the end of that piece every time we played it during tour or at our spring concerts. The piece ends with most of the ringers shaking a note for a long time to make a big finish. DP would bring his hands down while we were still ringing and do things like look at his watch to make fun of how long we were holding the note. Often, he'd just let us hold the note as he stepped off the podium and walked off the stage like he was just going to leave us there hanging on forever. Sometimes he'd even leave the room, but he'd come back a minute later and finally cut us off, which always drew laughter and applause from the crowd because they had no idea it was part of the performance.

One of the other things that got a big laugh when we started to encore that piece was that DP would remove his tuxedo jacket like he was really getting down to business. That in and of itself was funny, but then the audience would see the pink flamingo (the mascot of the group) embroidered on the back of his shirt. The crowds loved that. Flamingos eventually made their way to the shirts of all of the male members of the choir and beyond. When DP turned 50, the choir gleefully flamingoed his yard. Since then, the flamingo phenomenon has only continued to grow. The choir now has flamingoes of all varieties—Beanie Babies, stuffed flamingoes, blow-up flamingoes—on display at every concert except Christmas Candlelights.

DP also created a tradition during those Candlelight Services that he called the Ringing in of Christmas, and it set Bucknell's services apart from those of other universities or churches. After that catchy performance of "Festive Dance," we left the chapel with our bells while the choir singers and the congregation sang "Silent Night." With the help of many volunteer ringers, we moved stealthily around the inside and outside of the chapel (in December, in choir robes and dress shoes) to position ourselves in the four upper and lower corners of the space, trying desperately not to clang or accidentally ring a bell. The aim was to avoid being noticed at all.

As the congregation finished singing, the sanctuary drew dim and quiet. Finally, one low bell, a C2, chimed twelve, slow notes, metaphorically signaling midnight, the moment the day became Christmas. Once the chiming of that bell was complete, each set of bells, beginning with the lowest set, started ringing a peal, or a descending scale, of notes. As each group of bells began, the sound in the chapel grew bigger and fuller until all of the bells were randomly pealing at the same time.

It was at that point that DP began playing "Joy to the World" on the organ, and everyone began to sing. The sound coming from the inside of the chapel each time this happened was almost ethereal, like something I imagine coming from Heaven. It was celebratory and glorious and brought tears to my eyes as I took in the smell of the candles and the greens, and the sight of the beautiful lights, the talented Chapel Choir leading the singing, and DP at the organ. So many voices and instruments together to celebrate the season in one of the most beautiful places. From the first year on, this was my signal that Christmas was upon us, and it will forever be imprinted on my heart as such.

We performed those services three or four times every year, each to a chapel packed shoulder to shoulder with students, Bucknell faculty and staff, and hundreds of people from the town of Lewisburg and beyond. The services were so popular that Bucknell had to develop a ticket process and limit so that everyone who wanted to could attend. Tickets were free but were gone in a matter of minutes as soon as they were opened to the public. The extra preparation that went into these services was extraordinary, especially given that they occurred right after Thanksgiving but before winter break, in a time that also consisted of end-of-semester assignments, finals, and packing to go home. It was a stressful time, for sure, but man, did we have fun.

No matter how much was going on, there was never too little time to laugh about a wardrobe malfunction or play a joke on someone, usually DP. I quickly learned that it was a tradition among the upperclassmen to prank DP during performances. Often, this meant one of them sneaking up to the podium after rehearsal but before service to stick photos of questionably covered women into DP's music.

Once I became aware of this, I watched for it with great curiosity (and a little trepidation in case the upperclassmen couldn't be trusted and we were all about to get in trouble). But when DP turned the relevant sheet in his music, it was obvious he'd had a lot of practice at this. There was surprise and shock on his face when he saw a picture of a scantily clad woman, but only we could see that. Like a true professional, he quickly turned the page and put a big smile on his face, signaling to us that though we may have surprised him, he was unflappable. He clearly wanted to laugh, but he held it in, as did the rest of us, since we had to ready ourselves to play our next piece. Easier said than done if we were playing something like "O Come, O Come Emmanuel" or "What Child Is This?" Try as we might, we almost never shook him.

We only got ourselves into trouble once. Our Candlelight Services had become so popular that our local PBS TV station began filming them every four years to air on PBS stations around the state and country. Tapings were very fun, but also very stressful. There was so much extra equipment that had to be arranged, all of us had to remember we could be on camera at any second so we had to be on our best behavior, and it was a little bit intimidating to be in the middle of a song when a boom camera came swinging by our faces. These tapings were a hassle for DP because they added a layer of stress each year we were filmed, but they were also pretty cool because we could all tune in on Christmas Eve to see *A Bucknell Candlelight Christmas*.

They filmed us my junior year. The tradition of adding questionable photos to DP's music was going strong, and the guys were not going to let a taping get in the way. That was all well and good, but what they forgot was that not only do we have balconies in the chapel but also that the boom camera was catching everything, including passes over DP's music.

I'd almost forgotten about the tradition with all of the other chaos going on. But when DP turned to his music, I remembered—and for the first time I saw panic cross his face. And yet, he was so damn solid, even while being filmed. We registered his consternation, but no one else could see it, and without missing a moment, off we went into our first piece.

Afterward, words were had with the guys, reminding them that we were taping and, um, that's not acceptable for PBS. However, most of the time he let them do as they wished as long as they weren't hurting anyone, and more times than not, we laughed and laughed together. I still giggle thinking about those moments.

One of the coolest parts of that first semester was learning what I was capable of. I was reading and playing difficult music at a very high level. I was playing with good accuracy and tremendous musicality. Practice was a huge part of that, but the biggest factor was DP's nurturing.

DP didn't demand respect or excellence, he commanded it. He treated us as capable musicians, and he made the effort to get to know each of us as people. He learned what we were studying and what our extracurriculars were, and he learned about our families. He understood the stressful lives of college students, and he empathized with what we all had to deal with at any given time. However, he also expected that the time we spent in rehearsal was time completely committed and dedicated to ringing bells and ringing them well. The music he put in front of us was almost always challenging, but he only put it in front of us because he knew we could rise to the occasion. He believed we could accomplish difficult music, and because he believed in us, we believed in ourselves. Because he would look at us and say, "I know you can do this," we knew we could do it too.

If one of us struggled with something during rehearsal, he tried his best to help us but never pushed beyond what we were capable of in that moment. If a difficult section wasn't going to be mastered that night, he let us take it home and practice it instead of humiliating us in front of our peers. He gave us as much positive feedback as he could, often exclaiming in a gut reaction, "Yes, yes! That's it. That's exactly how I want it." We all felt so proud in those moments, and those moments are the ones that pushed us forward, kept us focused, and kept us motivated to do our best. We quickly learned that disappointing DP was worse than disappointing our own parents. We wanted to do our best for him because he wasn't only our director, he was our professor, our mentor, and our friend.

3

A Quirky Instrument

Without music,
life would be a mistake.
—Friedrich Nietzsche

We've become so accustomed to the sound of bells in our lives that we often don't even notice them anymore. And when we do, it's usually just to respond in the ways we've trained ourselves to without really paying much attention to the bell itself. Just this morning, I awoke to my alarm, heard the microwave beeping to remind me that I'd reheated my tea at least twice, and heard my car ding, telling me my keys were still in it while I was trying to lock it. And I'm not the only one who's conditioned to respond. Every time our dog hears a doorbell, whether on TV or in real life, he gives a big, deep bark that sometimes accidentally comes out like a whiny howl.

Bells are everywhere, from our homes and our phones to our vehicles, schools, and even workplaces. They wake us up. They remind us of things. They let us know when our food is ready and alert us when we leave our headlights on.

They're in our culture, in music and movies. The Salvation Army bell. The Monty Python bell telling people to "bring out your dead," and the line from *It's a Wonderful Life* that tells us that "every time a bell rings, an angel gets its wings." We're always reminded of bells at Christmas, whether in "Carol of the Bells" or "Jingle Bells" or church bells ringing on Christmas morning. Just the other day, I heard a Disney World commercial whose nod to Christmas was adding the transformative sound of sleigh bells to the classic "Heigh-Ho (it's off to work we go)" Snow White song.

Bells have long brought or summoned people together. Town criers shared news by ringing their bells, and bells signaled the call to dinner or worship. In our own nation's history, bells have called lawmakers to meetings and citizens to hear proclamations (the Liberty Bell and others). Bells have become a universal means of warning, telling many people at a time over long distances that there's a threat—an enemy coming, a fire happening, or a tornado bearing down. Where I live, we even have alarms for nuclear meltdown, which I hope we never have to use for more than practice.

While bells were originally created for utility, they quickly became sources of enjoyment and symbols for celebration, like church bells, wedding bells—and handbells. Bells rung by hand have been around since ancient times in many different cultures to signal and attract attention. The first set of tuned handbells appeared in England in the 17th century. In those days, sets of bells were rung in bell towers of churches and cathedrals by teams of people who took turns ringing the bells in a mathematical pattern called change ringing, which is an art in and of itself.

Housed in damp, cold bell towers (think *The Hunchback of Notre Dame*), these bells were quite loud since they needed to be heard for miles—and that meant they were also challenging to practice without disturbing entire towns. Out of necessity for a way to practice, smaller bells were created, tuned to a seven-note scale and fitted with leather handles. That allowed bell ringers to practice, sheltered from the elements in a normal-sized room.

Even though handbells were designed for the practice of tower ringing, people soon began playing tunes on them. They became more popular in 18th-century England when their range was expanded to twelve-note chromatic octaves, making it a lot easier to play recognizable tunes.

It was P. T. Barnum who brought handbells to the United States. The circus owner heard the Lancashire Bell Ringers while living in England and arranged to bring them to the US for a concert tour. Because he re-named the performers the Swiss Bell Ringers, most people mistakenly thought handbells came from Switzerland. They became popular in vaudeville, which is where they were played most often until the early 20th century.

In 1923, Margaret Shurcliff formed the first group of handbell ringers at a church in Boston. She'd learned the art of ringing alongside her father when she traveled with him to England to learn how to change ring. She became the first American woman to ring a peal (an entire change-ringing mathematical sequence) on tower bells in England—the vocation consisted entirely of men at the time. She returned to the US with a small set of Whitechapel handbells, the first of many handbells to make their way to this country. With those, she formed a small group of ringers that consisted mostly of her own children. I love handbells, but I'd have to pass on having enough children to form my own choir.

Margaret Shurcliff made these bell "bands" popular among her friends, and eventually New England. She went on to found the New England Guild of English Handbell Ringers, Inc. (NEGEHR), which became the American Guild of English Handbell Ringers, Inc. (AGEHR) in 1954. In 2010, after decades of growth and gains in popularity for handbells, AGEHR became Handbell Musicians of America (HMA), which is the national organization devoted to handbell ringing. Its mission is dedicated to advancing the musical art of handbell/handchime ringing through education, community, and communication.

Without being aware of any of that history, I had the privilege of actually seeing and ringing a tower bell on my first winter tour with the Rooke Chapel Ringers. It's still one of the coolest things I've ever done. We took a tour of the National Cathedral in Washington, DC, a new and beautiful experience to me in and of itself. The most intriguing and exciting part, at least to us ringers, was that we didn't just see the public areas of the cathedral. We climbed several flights of a secret, narrow staircase tucked away and closed off to the general public. We huffed and puffed up, up, and up into the bell tower, the highest point of the cathedral.

It was magical up there. There was a roof but no walls, so even though it was a cloudy, damp January day, we could see for miles. We learned all about the history of the bell tower and the amazing bell in it. It's a modern-day version of those gigantic bells that started change-ringing so long ago. Like its ancestors, this bell was designed to be rung by one person pulling a huge rope. That can still be done, but nowadays, most bells like this are run by motors driven by computers that ring the bells at the touch of a button. Bell automation means people don't have to go up into those freezing bell towers and pull heavy ropes anymore—but it's awfully fun to do.

It requires a lot of strength too. Through a pulley system, one person pulls a rope, allowing the bell to swing back and forth to ring. There's an additional rope attached to the top of the bell that hangs down when the bell is silent and flies up when the bell is in motion. We each got a turn to "ride" that rope as the bell was in motion. We had to have a tight grip—it picked us right up off the ground and swung us into the air! Even though we watched each other do it, it was still startling when it was our turn to fly. It was exhilarating to be lifted up by this huge metal object designed only to make a sound, not to act as an amusement for unsuspecting college kids. It was especially shocking for those of us dressed in skirts. Even now, I sometimes get shivers remembering that experience. After all, it's a pretty exclusive club of people who have ridden the bell at the National Cathedral.

Although most handbell ringers haven't had the opportunity to ride a tower bell, they have become very dedicated and enthusiastic about making handbell music. One of the main factors in the rise in popularity of handbells was the tremendous growth of mainline Protestant churches in the last third of the 20th century. People were flocking to churches throughout the US, and handbell programs began to spring up across the country. These handbell choirs would play in churches, enhancing Sunday worship and providing another way to glorify God. Occasionally, several of these choirs would meet and play together for the sheer enjoyment of it, creating the first handbell festivals.

Today, you can find handbell festivals all over the country, some sponsored directly by the Handbell Musicians of America and some sponsored by the local area districts of HMA. As ringers, we love to get together and play for a day, often putting on a concert at the end of the day to showcase our work. Though it's tiring to stand for eight hours of rehearsal and then perform a concert, those festivals and concerts help mainstream the instrument, drawing more people to the beauty of handbell music.

Though there are many people throughout the world who don't know what a handbell is, the instrument is indeed gaining recognition and popularity, thanks in part to composers who have spent countless hours arranging popular, well-known music for handbell choirs who then share them with the community. This is particularly true when trying to get young people excited about the instrument. After all, what kid—or adult, for that matter—wouldn't get excited at the prospect of playing an arrangement of one of Lady Gaga's songs or a popular Disney or Broadway tune? *Pirates of the Caribbean,* Adele, and the Beatles sound pretty cool on handbells.

In addition, masters of the handbell community have led the charge in trying to make the instrument more mainstream. David Weck, the founder and retired director of the Agape Ringers in the Chicago suburbs as well as a music editor for Hope Publishing Company, has called for handbell groups to play in larger venues, potentially partnering with other musicians in order to share the joy of handbells and bring more performers into the genre. As a prominent staple of the handbell community, Weck was featured in the *Chicago Tribune*'s article, "Bandleader wants bigger venues for bells."

Weck said, "Most handbell choirs perform in churches, and that's fine. But as with any art, you want to take it to the next level. We would like to do our concertizing not only in churches but also in concert halls and at fine arts events.... I don't know that we absolutely need to work with other instruments, but as an educator I know how important it is to vary the concerts in order to reach a broader audience."

As the national organization for handbell enthusiasts, HMA has created new programs and fresh excitement around the instrument through education and opportunities for new ringers to learn the craft. In recent years, HMA has hosted ringing events like the College Ring-In for college students and recent alumni to ring with a master conductor and prepare a concert over a weekend's time. It also hosts Distinctly Teen, a similar event focused on young musicians in grades 8-12 to gain experience and musicianship because we know that in order for something to really gain traction as something cool, it's got to start with our kids.

In addition to its other annual events that include Distinctly Bronze, there are events on the East and West coasts, new virtual offerings such as member chats and handbell happy hours, and a large National Seminar each summer in a different US city. These seminars are essentially the equivalent of every handbell geek's (yes, we proudly call ourselves geeks) dream conference. There are hundreds of ringers who come together to take classes, give and listen to concerts, make connections, and see old friends.

As with almost every other organization in the summer of 2020, last year's seminar had to be held online for the first time due to the COVID-19 pandemic. The HMA did a fabulous job of pivoting to make as much as possible happen online, and although it wasn't nearly the same as seeing each other in person, all of us ringers had chances to connect and learn together virtually, which was actually pretty fun. Of course we're all very much looking forward to an in-person seminar in 2021 in Phoenix as well as the International Handbell Symposium in 2022 in Nashville. Handbells are popular not just in the US but also all over the world.

HMA is also a benevolent organization with a grant program for qualifying applicants to encourage and support creative projects, all with the mission of advancing the art of handbell/handchime ringing through education, community, and communication. Over the years, the AGEHR Grant Fund has given thousands of dollars to individuals, organizations, and subgroups of the HMA for projects in research and education, projects benefitting underserved populations, formal education, and handbells for special groups.

The Veterans Bridge to Recovery Program at the Minneapolis VA Health Care System serves thousands of veterans and demonstrates the healing power of music and handbells. Many veterans suffer from mental health challenges and the mistaken belief that they can't learn new things, whether that's life skills or otherwise. Many have specifically been told that they can't learn to play an instrument, which is a shame because music, in many forms, can be therapeutic. VBR applied for a grant from HMA in 2012 to start a music therapy program in which veterans would learn to play handchimes.

The group was unsure of their ability and whether they would have any fun at all, especially without a conductor, but they quickly found their groove working as a team to select music, name the chimes for easier playing, write in counting and cues, and learn to set everything up and put it away, caring for all of the equipment properly. The choir taught the group responsibility and how to set and achieve goals. The grant allowed the group to purchase the chimes, music, and equipment, and the group named itself the Ringing Cavaliers.

The Ringing Cavaliers became an outreach vehicle for the Veterans Bridge to Recovery program by playing concerts and going into the community to provide hope and support to others who face mental health challenges. Jenny Cauhorn, former Executive Director of HMA, told me that the grant and subsequent story was probably the most meaningful one throughout her time at HMA. "One player reached out with a thank you note saying how grateful he was for the group," she told me. "For the first time in his life, he was a musician when everyone else had told him he would never be capable of being one."

This and other HMA outreach and activities are in order to increase interest in and excitement for handbells and handbell music. It works because handbells truly are somewhat unique, but without being too weird or inaccessible.

I think that's another reason I love handbells so much. They aren't a mainstream musical instrument, much like my own first name isn't very common. Before Hillary Clinton, the name Hillary wasn't really synonymous with any particular person, personality, or expectations. No one has preconceived notions of what a Hillary can or should do. The name is slightly unique but not unpronounceable or strange. Everyone knows about the piano and instruments of the orchestra, particularly those like flute and violin. But not everyone knows about handbells, just like not everyone knows a Hillary. Maybe it was bound to happen, a girl named Hillary falling for an unusual instrument like handbells. Or maybe I just like surprising people with what I can do and what I love.

4

The Power
of the Music

*Music ... can name the unnameable
and communicate the unknowable.*
—Leonard Bernstein

So what is it about these bells? What's the draw, the thing that keeps us coming back? They're definitely beautiful instruments, and they make beautiful music. But why do tens of thousands of us geek out over them?

Those of us who ring feel very strongly about what we do. It brings us such joy and fulfillment that we are all eager to share it with others. Because even people who know about handbells may not know what they can do, it's great fun to surprise an audience with all of the cool sounds bells can make and the interesting ways they can be played. They're both auditory and visual, giving the audience more than one way to take in what's happening.

Playing bells also stokes my own passion for education because each audience learns something new about this remarkable instrument. Even if someone doesn't take up the instrument simply because of hearing us play, we like to think we've introduced them to something new, something they might find joy in. We hope that our passion for what we do can be transferred to them through our musicality and enthusiasm.

DP fell in love with bells because of their musical range and their sound. He told me, "I love how bells affect audiences, particularly when they hear familiar music played in an interesting style. I've gotten notes in the mail from strangers, one in particular that said, 'I've never heard bells like that before,' and that's what sticks. When there's a feeling (that) the audience is with you, and they really get it."

Not only is there the education and joy, but the mechanics of bells are different than any other instrument, which is as intriguing to ringers as it is to audiences. On paper, handbells are the only instrument besides piano for which each ringer is reading the entire score of music. If we play a part in an orchestra, we get handed our own instrument's part and no one else's. When we play bells, each person has a copy of the entire piece of music, every part included. It looks exactly like what we would see if we sat down to play something on a piano—all of the parts together at once. However, unlike a pianist who's playing all of those notes, each handbell ringer has to pick out her own few notes among the rest of them and has to continue doing that to play through the entire piece.

For other musicians, that might seem an odd way to read music, especially given that when playing together, ringers have to both ignore and be aware of their neighbor's notes at the same time. Since ringers sometimes have to share bells, we must be cognizant of what's happening in our neighbor's parts but not so much that it distracts us from where our notes fit in the rhythm. A ringer cannot simply play in a vacuum with her head focused solely on her part, and yet accuracy of notes and rhythm for each part is essential.

"It's a balance of individuality and the importance of the individual to the group," says esteemed conductor and composer Cathy Moklebust. "When you have twelve or thirteen people playing the same instrument it's unique, but when only one person is on each part, there is more onus on the individual musician because you're not dependent on a section of people playing or singing the same part as you and that part is so much more integral to the whole than if you're one of eight flute players, for example."

As a percussionist herself, Moklebust was drawn to handbells because another one of their unique attributes is their physicality and similarity to percussion instruments. As she explains, "Handbells are very physical in nature. They are played with the ringers standing, they require extensive use of the shoulders, arms, wrists, and hands, and all of that requires good posture."

Handbells require a lot of movement from side to side as well as standing for many hours at a time, which is very tiring even though we aren't walking anywhere. They also require a ton of equipment (tables, foam pads, tablecloths, the bells, music stands and binders, and all kinds of fun extras like mallets, choir chimes, and even sticks of wood) and lots of preparation and clean up. Surely those things make them unique, but they're not among the reasons why I continue to play handbells. After all, most of us could do without all of the schlepping, sore muscles, blisters, and inevitable inclement weather when all of that stuff needs to be unloaded and reloaded. All of us have had that day when the weather has been beautiful and suddenly turns lousy as soon as it's time to load or unload bells.

There's a fascinating hypothesis that says bells have become so innately ingrained in us that our bodies produce an automatic physical reaction to bells. As I've mentioned, bells have historically signaled humans to come together in one way or another. Native Americans have used bells in their dress, song, and celebration; finger cymbals and bells are common in Spanish dance. We've made entire songs for Christmas about bells. Bells have even allowed us to stay connected to animals. Cows wear bells to let farmers know where they are, we put bells on the collars of our cats and dogs, and even horses wear bells for utility and decoration. There are so many ways we've become conditioned to bells that it's possible we've developed unconscious reactions to them.

Musically, it's interesting to ponder the attraction of handbells, especially given their resonating nature. Perhaps it's the actual vibration of the instrument that draws us in. We ringers can certainly feel that throughout our bodies when we play, and we hope our audiences can feel it too.

One brilliant example of both musicality and the way these bells physically affect us is The Joybells, the choir at a nonprofit educational organization in Pennsylvania called Melmark that serves children and adults with autism and other challenges. The Joybells is the adult handbell choir in which adults with developmental disabilities, including deafness, get to share in the joy of playing bells. The choir has played at White House events, a gubernatorial inauguration, and Philadelphia Phillies games.

For there to be people who choose to play an instrument without being able to hear it, there must be something that speaks to one of the other senses. There must be something powerful enough about playing the handbells to engage people who cannot even hear them the way you and I can. Brian Childers, the director of music for children and youth music and handbells at Myers Park United Methodist Church in Charlotte, North Carolina, and music advisor at Handbell Musicians of America, definitely thinks there's something special about handbells.

"There's something about the sound of bells that people literally resonate with," he says. "They feel it deep in their bodies, which is why so many people who start ringing bells continue for the rest of their life. There's something about the sound of bells that people connect with in a very personal way."

Whether the resonance of bells is literal or figurative, it was at work during Rooke Chapel Ringer bell tours, a ringer's dream come true that involved playing bells for days on end. We played concerts for the churches or high schools of each of our senior members as our way to give back to the programs that had started many of us on our bell journeys. Tour was usually a four- to six-day trip up and down the Mid-Atlantic. It was rare and very special if we got to fly somewhere further away, as that posed challenges both monetarily and logistically. It meant we either had to ship our bells (slightly risky and very expensive) or fly them with us.

Shipping would mean sending each individual case—perhaps combining only the smallest cases into a box or two—with precautions like lots of bubble wrap and padding, even though the bells would be nested snugly in their velvet-lined padded cases. They would need to be insured in case they got damaged, and that would be prohibitive given that the current retail price of a set of five-octave bells with cases is about $27,000. Even twenty years ago, that would still have been a significant amount of money. I know we'd be praying the entire time that the bells would make it to our destination and back without major damage. I can just see, in my mind's eye, some shipping clerk hurling a bell case onto a conveyor belt with a thud. Just the idea of cracking a bell makes my chest constrict.

Carrying them with us and checking them would cause the same headaches. It would be very difficult to ensure their safety, and my guess is that the airlines would be happy to charge a tremendous sum for a set of equipment weighing roughly a combined 310 pounds. I also can't imagine how fifteen of us could work it out to check our own luggage and about twenty cases of bells.

When we did indeed travel by air, we ended up borrowing bells from the church at our destination, a much safer and cheaper alternative. Given these restraints, more often than not, we took off for destinations within driving distance for a several-day voyage of eating, sleeping, and ringing.

In the early days, we traveled in two fifteen-passenger vans: one loaded with all of us and the second loaded with all of our stuff. We even used walkie-talkies to communicate, for real. This was pre-cell phone era, and apparently it was pre-liability era too. Can you imagine a college junior or senior driving fourteen other college kids around the northeast US with the chaperone following in a separate van carrying about $20,000 dollars' worth of equipment? And while we were all very reliable and serious about our safety and responsibilities, one might have questioned that, considering some of our walkie-talkie conversations.

One year, there was a ringer in the group whom we'll call Stacy. Stacy loved to tell stories in the style of Michelle in the movie *American Pie,* whose every anecdote began with: "This one time, at band camp …" Stacy talked incessantly and always tried to outdo everyone else's stories, leading the rest of us to begin every walkie-talkie conversation by bragging, "I have an uncle who …" She never caught on to the joke.

Tour was the best time of the year, with lots of connection, lots of eating, and lots of ringing. We stayed with families who volunteered to host us for overnights and meals, and we rang bells for hours on end as we rehearsed for our upcoming concerts. We talked and laughed and had fun—even when so much togetherness and a tight schedule occasionally lent itself to some irritability.

After the concerts, we'd change our clothes and then pack up and carry all of our equipment back to our van. In and out, we'd pass each other carrying out cases and tables and coming back empty-handed for more. There was a particular way to load the van so that everything fit, and everyone knew the drill: big cases first, then tables, then other cases, then foam, music stands, and everything else.

Bucknell was lucky enough to have some extra bells. We always packed them just in case, since we never knew how we were going to be able to set up for each performance. However, we didn't always have room for all of the extra bell cases, and so we had to pack each extra bell separately, very carefully. One dark January night when I was serving as manager of the group, I was making one of my last trips out to the van when I noticed the guys were finished and closing the side door. Someone had something to add in, and one of the guys reopened that door.

That's when it happened. One of the extra bells tumbled right out of the door and smack down onto the asphalt of the parking lot.

I, for lack of better description, lost my shit. I tore into the two guys who were loading the van, demanding to know why in the world that bell was so precariously placed. Did they not know how much these things cost? I'm pretty sure I told them if that ever happened again I would take their loading privileges away. And I think I made my point that they weren't being careful enough because they both stood there, frozen and shame-faced, staring at me. I grabbed the bell and inspected it—luckily no damage was done. I handed it back and told them to put it away the right way, finish up, and get in the other van, fast.

Unbeknownst to me, DP's wife, Ruth, was watching the incident unfold. To this day, she remembers how hard I was on those two when that bell took a spill. She tells me that she never worried when I was in charge because I wasn't afraid to lay down the law. I'm pretty sure from then on, both of those guys were slightly afraid of me, and what's more is that I was okay with that. I didn't mind being a hardass to protect the very expensive equipment we had the privilege to use.

We had some great educational experiences together on those trips, like riding the bell at the Cathedral and touring the Schulmerich handbell factory in Hatfield, Pennsylvania. There are two handbell-making companies in the US, both in Pennsylvania. Schulmerich is the larger of the two, but I have to admit that of the two producers, I was a Malmark snob before I got to use Schulmerich bells for the first time, which was at least a year after we toured the Schlumerich factory. Every ringer has her own preference, but we started with Malmark bells at Bucknell, and so when we got to tour Schulmerich, I was only sort of excited. It turned out to be completely intriguing, seeing exactly how each part of each bell is crafted so very carefully from bronze, and with a tour group our size, we got to ask a lot of questions and glean a lot of information.

One of the many things we learned was that a handbell will never go out of tune unless it gets damaged. The bells never have to be re-tuned like a piano. They will always retain their exact sound because that's based on the thickness and shape of the bronze. However, they do require some maintenance. There are a lot of small screws holding the handles together, and lots of intricacies that make the clappers move only in the forward and backward direction. If the casting (the bronze part) of the bell does get cracked or otherwise broken, it can't be fixed. It can only be replaced by a new one.

In other words, everyone should insure their bells.

I'm now completely a Schulermich bell snob. I've grown to like the tone of them, the more comfortable handles, and that sleek look of all black handles as opposed to Malmark, which alternates white and black.

Handbell ringers often refer to their choirs or groups as families because really, that's what we become, especially when we travel together. Nothing brings people closer together than eating, sleeping, and traveling together 24/7, not to mention doing the same schlepping of the equipment over and over again. When we were in such close quarters, we really got to know each other, sometimes more than we wanted to. We got to know each other's families and friends, college experiences, and hometowns. We learned each other's quirks and food preferences, and sometimes even medical needs and bathroom habits, although I'm sure we all could have gone without knowing the latter. We also learned to read each other's moods, lift each other up when we were down, and let each other rest when we needed space.

Brian Childers weighed in on this as well: "I think hand-bells teach us more about connection than any other musical genre except possibly choral music. You play the same music but everyone has their own part, so there is a high level of trust. That's one of the reasons I try with my groups to give them as many opportunities to be together when they're not ringing as possible—any time, and this transcends age, they are together before, after, or during rehearsal, it makes the ringing better. It is more like family." We were indeed, more like a family.

We also had the unique opportunity to get to know DP better. This felt satisfyingly special because, technically, he was a professor of ours, and none of us ever got to travel with or spend so much time with other professors. We learned when we could have fun with him, when we could joke and get silly, and when he meant business. We knew when we could tease him or make fun of him and when to knock it off. After all, it couldn't all be business when traveling with a man who took his nickname so tongue-in-cheek seriously that his car's license plate read "DEEPEE."

DP always joined us for dinner, and it became a fun and sometimes repetitive game to predict what we would be eating. Every time we played a concert, the church or organization hosting us would feed us beforehand. There are only so many things that are convenient to serve a large group, so we ate a lot of lasagna, pasta, casseroles, and sandwiches. Anything other than those entrees, like make-your-own fajitas, was a welcome surprise.

After every concert, there was a reception, also hosted by the church and always lovely. But it was after Christmas, and every reception was as predictable as the last: cookies and juice, cookies and juice, cookies and, oooh, punch! More than once I heard DP say, "If I have to eat another cookie or brownie, I'm going to vomit," or "I'd so much rather have wine." As much as we enjoyed eating—we joked that we'd end up rolling home—most of us never wanted to see another Christmas cookie again each year after tour.

The thing that brought us closest together was the nature of the music and the instrument, the fact that each person plays her own unique part as an integral and necessary part of the whole. In that way, handbell choirs are more like sports teams than many other kinds of musical ensembles. On each sports team, each position has its role to play. If a player doesn't fulfill her role, the entire team suffers. The same happens with handbells.

David Harris, director of the Raleigh Ringers in North Carolina, mentions this team phenomenon. "I always think we are so reliant on each other, the whole team aspect of what we do," he says. "In Europe, they were called bell teams, and it really is a team sport because no one person controls playing the whole melody him/herself and you are reliant on your neighbors and the other members of your group to overcome challenges."

Anyone who's ever toured with a music group knows that one of the most fulfilling things that happens is that everyone's skill level accelerates exponentially, and the real, actual music begins to come out. When we spend days and days playing and rehearsing the same music, getting it in our heads and our hands and our bodies, the music starts to become a part of us. We've repeated the same patterns so often that muscle memory begins to take over.

For me, this kind of deepening usually happens around our third concert on a tour or our third day of ringing a festival, when the unconscious rhythm of the music truly seeps into my body and soul. Even if my brain went blank for a second, my body would take over and do what it was trained to do. My hands would keep going, ringing, damping, and grabbing the next bell or turning the page. It becomes so ingrained that I could probably play at least parts of pieces in my sleep, knowing through every song what comes next and then what follows that.

The entire process of getting to this point is fascinating, watching what the brain and body can do after a certain amount of time and practice. It astonished me when I mastered some difficult part, either with a lot of note changes or difficult rhythm. I remember this kind of "clicking" happening in my brain when I first mastered "Festive Dance," the piece that became our signature piece and poses a tempo challenge for almost every ringer position. This one is unique because each year, as new members join the choir, they learn the piece for the first time, whereas anyone returning has already mastered at least one part of it.

That moment when, as a new ringer, I mastered my part—particularly the section where the notes whiz by on the page—felt like I had won the lottery. I was so proud and so happy to have gotten to that place with that particular piece because it felt like an inauguration, a final acceptance into the group. I felt I was truly a Rooke Chapel Ringer when I could play "Festive Dance." It certainly helped that the song was such a crowd pleaser.

This kind of leveling up isn't just mechanically and physically satisfying. It's also an intense, emotional experience—at least, it is for me. I intuitively begin to feel what's next in the music. Pieces come together in a such a way that they are seamless and all-consuming. The notes swirl in my head when I'm awake, when I'm asleep, and when I'm thinking of other things. I fall asleep with a song in my head, wake up with another, and hum the tunes all day long.

All of us ringers complain about musical ear worms, but I actually love it. It's an intoxicating, addicting feeling, like an incredible high. It's as if the music settles into every part of my body, mind, and soul. It feels like accomplishment and comfort and excitement all at the same time. It's one of the most powerful feelings I've ever had, and I'm incredibly grateful for having had the opportunity to experience it so many times.

It's been a long time since I've played music on my own, and though I could probably get a similar sense of accomplishment mastering a flute solo, it's a special thing when this kind of feeling is shared within a group. When the music is that good and it's gelled that well together, it's a shared triumph. It's something very special, a bond I can only get from playing those bells with other talented people. It's a connection between the musicians and the notes, the musicians and each other, and musicians and the conductor.

In almost all of our discussions, DP and I return again and again to this feeling, trying to name it, categorize it, or qualify it in some way. In a recent conversation, he wondered aloud whether this feeling could be likened to that of elite athletes: "Is this what Olympians feel, this high, this adrenaline, chemical and emotional reaction, a euphoria of sorts?"

I can't say I'll ever be able to compare the two, but to me it's almost like a secret too good to share. Well, maybe a secret that you give part of to the audience and keep the rest for yourself.

DP, as is often the case, says it best: "This is the amazing mystery behind these reverberating objects ... they reach inside one's soul and open an inward feeling or emotion that is sometimes inexpressible."

5

What We Love
Is Always Worth It

*The happiness of a man in this life
does not consist in the absence
but in the mastery of his passions.*
—Alfred Lord Tennyson

In the summer of 2013, twelve years after I graduated from Bucknell, my phone rang. It was a wonderful surprise to hear DP's voice on the other end. Although we'd become good friends and had stayed in touch over the years, I wasn't expecting his call. I certainly wasn't anticipating the request he was going to make.

The Rooke Chapel Ringers, he told me, were in a tough place. He didn't expect there would be enough students auditioning to fill all the spaces the graduating seniors had just left behind, and he wanted me to consider the idea of joining the bell choir for the year if he needed me for one of those spots.

Me? Really!?

I was thrilled—I missed ringing terribly—and I was quite honored. I knew he asked me because I was a solid ringer who was dependable and dedicated. We only live about seventy-five minutes from Bucknell, a doable commute for a weekly practice and monthly performance.

This would be DP's last year before retirement, and it would be a privilege to be part of his last choir at Bucknell. But I was also now a mom of two young girls with a husband who worked retail hours and almost never had a Thursday (the evening of their rehearsal) off. This gave me pause, but I told DP I would think about it because oh, how I would love to do it!

I had to think about how this would work out with my family. They were my life, and save for the few hours a month I worked from home either writing grants or training adult English as a Second Language teachers, I spent all my time with them. I hadn't made a commitment this big since before I'd had kids, and it was going to take some sacrifice on everyone's part.

I'd be gone every Thursday from 3:30 to 10 p.m., one Sunday morning and afternoon a month, and then many performance evenings in December. This meant hiring babysitters, missing meals and bedtimes, and probably skipping out on some sleep. It meant letting someone else oversee what my kids ate for dinner and how they behaved. It meant my husband was on solo duty when he got home from a full day's work. Most of all, it meant things at home might not be exactly as I would have them.

For a fleeting moment, all of this seemed like a lot of sacrifice—until I remembered how much I'd loved those three years ringing at Bucknell and how much I'd loved ringing for DP. He's one of the most revered conductors and composers in the bell world, and I have the utmost respect and love for him. He has taught, and continues to teach, not only about handbells but also the greater messages of music, such as communication and connection. The opportunity to go back to Bucknell and ring as an adult was something I knew I'd regret passing up.

More significantly, the prospect of playing bells every week for nine months made me so giddy I couldn't stop smiling. It was a passion I'd ignored and been willing to sacrifice for years between graduating, moving, and starting a family.

For over a decade there had been reasons why joining a handbell choir wasn't a top priority. Sometimes I couldn't find a good enough group, sometimes my job kept me too busy, sometimes new babies kept me from doing anything I was passionate about, including sleeping. I could have made quick work of some of those excuses, but instead I'd put my passion on the back burner, just simmering there and waiting for me to turn up the heat or move it to the front of the stove. Instead of acknowledging it as something that fed my soul and gave me energy, I viewed it as a selfish luxury, something moms with young kids didn't get to do.

The social debates around the topic of mothers and families and the roles that women play are innumerable, and surely societal pressure factored into my decision. But in the end, it wasn't about that for me. It was about getting back to doing something I love. While I thought about how spending less time with my children would affect them, I also thought about how great it would be for them to see their mom doing something she was passionate about. I knew in my heart that following that passion and having that joy in my life would only make me better for them.

Two days later, my girls and I were getting ice cream when

my phone rang again—it was DP. I'll never forget that call because I was so hoping I would be needed. And it turns out, I was. I answered the phone, and DP said, "Hillary, I need you to play with us this year. I just don't have enough kids. Are you willing?"

Practically jumping out of my skin but trying to be nonchalant, I told him that I would be honored. He said that rehearsals started the next Thursday and I should plan to be there. I was so excited it felt like an electric current coursing through my body. I felt incredibly blessed, as most of us do when we get the opportunity to align with our passions. It's not just a fleeting feeling of happiness but rather an exhilaration, a brain, body, and soul knowing that what we're doing is what we're meant to do.

That next Thursday, walking onto the Bucknell campus and into that beautiful chapel I loved so much felt like coming home. It was like I'd never left, like I'd belonged there all my life. It was comforting and exciting at the same time. I smiled so hard my cheeks hurt, and said a silent prayer of gratitude for this opportunity that seemed to have come about through divine intervention.

Time had changed my perspective. I still remembered the worries, the drama, and the pressure of being a student. But here I was, with twelve years of jobs and marriage and children under my belt. I'd lost loved ones, gained experience, and begun to learn what was really important in life. I looked at things differently. I prayed I would continue to remember those times in school so I could empathize with the other ringers, students who were young enough (or was I old enough?) to be my children. I wanted to show interest in them and respect for their feelings and stage in life.

But given all that life experience, I wasn't sure how I was

going to fit in. Was I supposed to be cool? Was I supposed to befriend them? Or was I supposed to just play the role of old-head coming in and filling a spot? To me, that was much more nerve-racking than my ability to pick up the bells and play.

As it turned out, I had no reason to worry. The students were truly welcoming and excited to have me. I stayed out of their way at first, learning how they were used to setting up and tearing down, which big bells had to be retrieved from upstairs, and what extra stuff we needed. Slowly, I slid into the role of just-another-ringer, but also as a lucky overseer who didn't have to do all of the heavy lifting.

It was pretty perfect. The students knew I had a long drive on either end of rehearsal, so they almost never let me stay to put things away. They also didn't expect me to lug big bells or organize who was bringing the weekly snack, a ritual I quickly learned was a competition between Tostitos Lime (DP's favorite) and brownies (the ringers' preference). But because I knew the value of treats and my hometown was Hershey, I was not above winning them over with bags of chocolatey treats.

The students gave DP and me some space to talk—our conversations were often about boring adult things anyway—but also accepted me as part of their group. I'm an observer by nature, and I tend to hang back until I get a feel for a group. Here, I quietly got to know the ringers on my right and left and watched the way all of the personalities fit together before I started speaking up, and I think that earned me their respect. I came in with no expectations, no plans to try to change anything, no pretenses. I was simply thrilled to be a part of the group.

I also felt the responsibility of being an older, more experienced player who theoretically had more advanced ringing skills. That pressure to perform well felt a little heavy at first, but I knew in my heart that most of the stress was of my own making. After all, we were all starting musically on equal footing—the first rehearsal was the first time all of us were seeing the music. In the moments that shook my confidence, when I made mistakes or confused bells or forgot what a particular sign meant in the music, I tried to remember that DP had called me back to do this. He surely had other options, but he asked me. I could do this.

I took my music home to study every week, but some weeks, I got more studying done than others. I still had to take my daughter to preschool, keep the toddler occupied, and run a household. I remember frequently studying during my daughter's piano lesson because I got to sit quietly and uninterrupted for that half hour. Juggling my responsibilities as a parent with my commitment to the group was a challenge.

Given that, it was amusing to listen to the students describing how stressed they were, what their weeks looked like between rehearsals, classes, and extracurriculars. They were no slackers, for sure, and I remember feeling those feelings—like I had not enough time to do all I had to do, like my work was never going to get done, like there was no way I could handle classes and meetings and homework and summer job interviews.

It would have served no one for me to say, "Well, if you think you're busy now, wait until real life hits!" Admittedly, I did sometimes snicker to myself, reminding myself of the changes in perspective after twelve years, especially how our perceptions of busy or stressed or not having time for things are. There were times when the students would complain about being tired and I'd roll my eyes and think, "Really? You're tired? Dude, I've got two kids, a husband, and a household to run, and I'm driving three hours a week for rehearsal!"

It is a great challenge in life to fit a passion or some creativity into a full adult life. And in moments of overwhelm, the struggle might not seem worth it. But the truth is, once we get started, we remember how good it feels to get those things we love onto our to-do list of adult responsibilities. Once I got to rehearsal, once we played for an audience, once I got to know my fellow ringers, the joy I felt quashed the moments of fatigue and questioning whether it was worth it. It was.

That fall was marked by a something very special: the thirtieth anniversary of the Rooke Chapel Ringers. Since that coincided with DP's last year before retirement, he'd decided to hold a reunion for everyone who'd played for him, something that hadn't been done before. We had about fifty alumni of varying graduation years come back to campus for an entire weekend of rehearsal and festivities. As I signed people in, I recognized some names I'd only heard as legend, met some new faces, and gave out lots of hugs to ringers I'd played with.

We had enough ringers for three full choirs of bells, which was the largest number of bells I had heard played at once up to that point. I'd thought the music had filled the chapel before, but this was on a whole different scale. As we rehearsed Friday evening and Saturday morning, the sound went from impressive and just big to glorious and musical, both soft and loud, and so much like the way the Rooke Chapel Ringers always sounded.

It was also tremendous fun having so many former students there, sharing memories and laughs. Some of their best stories were about DP, whether they were seriously playing music or, as was often the case, playing a prank on him. It was that weekend I learned of the time they convinced him that the bells had been stolen. They'd worked together to move all of the equipment from its proper storage place, and then, when DP showed up for rehearsal, they claimed everything had been taken. Surprisingly, the jig went on for quite some time until DP, who'd really bought into the story, called campus security and the students gave up the joke before things got too serious. That story went down in Rooke Chapel Ringer history.

There was a fancy dinner with a slideshow and lots of special toasts, and then we played in the chapel that Sunday for all of the friends and families who came along. It was just like old times—but better. There were personalities who were as big or bigger than when they'd been students, and there were ringers who'd kept ringing and many who hadn't. It didn't matter once we were all playing together under DP's baton because he knew how to bring out the best in every musician, and we were home.

I think I had the luckiest vantage point of all because I was an alum who knew the "old days" and also a current ringer who got to give the scoop to the current choir. I got to assist DP with some of the logistics, and yet I wasn't stressed. I already knew the music because the current choir had prepared it. I felt like I had the most special role in the entire group—a unique link between the past and present, maybe even a teacher's pet of sorts. But it was DP, and I didn't care. If anyone wanted to fight me for that spot, I would take them down. That's how dedicated I was to that group and to this man.

Of course the entire weekend didn't go off without a hitch. We had to borrow bells from local churches to make sure we had enough for three choirs' worth of ringers, and so most of our bells were not our own. It's important to take care of your own bells, but it's really important to take care of someone else's. During Saturday's rehearsal, there were several male alums ringing behind me who were really enjoying themselves and having a great time, perhaps a little too much so. As they joked around, one of them knocked a bell right off the table. Smack! It landed loudly on the linoleum floor, and I swear all of the air was instantly sucked out of the vast space of the chapel.

I could see the anger flash in DP's eyes, and for a minute, his face told me he considered letting those guys really have it. He took a deep breath, clearly weighing his options, and then, having decided not to turn the whole morning sour, calmly but sternly asked if the bell was damaged. Luckily, it was not. He then curtly told the guys to knock it off and that if it happened again, they were out. Thankfully, the rest of rehearsal went on smoothly.

The Rooke Chapel Ringer 30th Reunion Ringers, Chapel service, October 2013

After that reunion, we went headlong into preparations for Christmas Candlelight Services, which required greater commitment. I had to be at Bucknell five nights one week, excluding Tuesday and Saturday. This was December in Central Pennsylvania, where the weather can be great or awful at a moment's notice. The first part of the week was uneventful, but by the time Friday evening came, the weather turned. I, along with several family members in other vehicles, drove up to Bucknell in what was a sloppy, drizzly, icy mess. I got there in one piece but was late due to traffic, which put a slight sense of panic in all of us. No one wants to start a series of performances with someone missing at the beginning of the rehearsal, and the missing person doesn't want to upset the group or feel rushed, and I certainly felt rushed. I had had no time to eat, and I was surprisingly nervous.

Upon arriving at the chapel, I was brought immediately back to the exciting and anxious feelings I had in college when family would visit and I would be showcasing something or another. Even though I was grown, and this was not my first performance or even Candlelight Service, this time meant just as much to me. I may have been even more nervous for this Candlelight Service than any I had as a student because I really felt (through no pressure from the ringers or DP, just my own) that I had to prove myself. I had to prove to myself that I could do this just as I had done years before, and in my mind, I needed to be better than I was as a student. After all, I was so much more experienced and older (although I had already heard compliments when playing with the ringers that I just looked like another student rather than a 35-year-old woman playing with the choir, which felt pretty good, of course).

The evening began, and we played our prelude. I relaxed as I was brought right back to the magic of those services, ushering the Christmas season in the only way that felt right. The glow of the lights in the chapel, the sound of the Rooke Chapel Choir singing, and the beauty of the Christmas story once again proved magical. My heart soared to be a part of it. I hadn't needed to worry; whatever mistakes I made went unnoticed by everyone except us ringers and DP, and the fun, camaraderie, and excitement of it always overpowered any nerves I had. Admittedly, there was also relief once all of my family got home safely that night because it was snowing like crazy by the time the service was over, which was surely very Christmas-like and serene, but also potentially dangerous.

DP and Ruth always hosted a Christmas party at their farm a short distance from campus after the final Candlelight Service. I'd had such fun at those parties in college. I knew I would have enjoyed it that much more as an adult—watching the college kids kicking back before the pressure of finals, relaxing with DP and Ruth in their cozy farmhouse, and drinking wine.

But this was perhaps one of the few times I felt my age and the life-stage difference between the ringers and me. While the ringers boarded the bus to go make merry, I got in my car to drive home yet again, my older eyes and body exhausted from all of the travel and hecticness of the last week. At this point, I really wanted to give more to my passion, to stay with everyone and build relationships, but my responsibilities won out. It was time to go home and acquiesce to my other roles in life. I was sad at the time, but party or not, I was so grateful to get home safe that night, and so thankful for the opportunity I had to again be a part of something that meant so much to me.

We didn't get to see each other for a month before it was time for tour in January. I must admit, I was again a little nervous—it was one thing to show up for rehearsals and performances, but it felt like another to travel with DP and a bunch of students when I was not a college kid anymore but also not a colleague of DP's. Where would I fit in? Where was I supposed to sit on the bus—with the students or DP? Was I supposed to socialize with the ringers or the adults at our homestays and meals?

As it happened, everything worked out just fine. I sat near the front of the bus with DP so we could sometimes chat, but I could still sleep when I needed to. Besides, I was no longer young enough to tolerate the motion of the back of the bus. And my homestays were great. That particular tour, we ended up pulling in another alumna to play with us on short notice when one of the students had to go abroad. So, for one of the homestays, she and I got to hang out, sleep in, and sit with our host family and drink coffee instead of going bowling with the students (which would have been totally fun, but even at 35, I didn't have the same stamina I did at 22).

It was, however, an incredible gift to get to know my fellow ringers. They were talented musicians and wicked smart students, many of them double majors whose fields of study ranged from engineering and biochemistry to business. I also got to listen in as they talked about how stressed they were about the upcoming semester, or, in the case of seniors, over the next steps of graduate school or work and how they'd find jobs. I promised myself I'd remember how pressured they felt and, even so, how very young they still were. I wanted to make sure I'm prepared to give my own kids the grace they'll need at that age as well as just enjoy them, because the kids were also silly, funny, and fun to be around.

We performed three concerts in five days, one of which I completely bombed. That night, it was like I was at the concert, but I wasn't. My head felt disconnected from what my body was doing, and the more I tried to correct myself, the more mistakes I made. And big ones, too. Wrong notes everywhere, coming in before or after I was supposed to, even confusing which bells I had in my hands. It was like I'd never seen the music even though we'd been playing all semester and for two days straight, right up until about two hours before the concert began.

At first I kept getting confused looks from DP, but after so many missteps, he just quit looking at me, knowing that I was well aware of how poorly I was doing. It was clearly an off night for me, something every musician has experienced at one point or another. Nothing came together, nothing gelled, nothing worked as it was supposed to.

I walked out of the first half of that concert straight to a water fountain, away from everyone, to get myself together and shake it off. I took a lot of deep breaths and gave myself a little talking to. "Get it together, Hillary," I said. "You can do this. You know how to do this."

I really had to remind myself that no matter how much I loved what I was doing, there were just times when I was going to be out of sync. Just because I was enjoying bells and even practicing hard didn't mean that everything would be perfect or even close. We can stumble at our passions just as we stumble at other things, and the important part is to just keep going. Even when we fall flat on our faces, we can get back up and try again.

Whatever I did during that intermission thankfully worked because I played much better the second half of our performance. I wouldn't say I completely redeemed myself, but I at least felt like I could get back on the bus with some of my dignity left.

The other concerts all went well, and as always happens, our music grew much tighter and more melodious, which was satisfying both from a musical perspective and a maturity perspective. The students had a great time and really took me in as one of their own. It was the same magic I'd experienced on other tours but had never appreciated as a college kid as much as I did now.

The spring semester came, and we got to travel again, this time to a festival in Ohio that DP was conducting. This was the first time he'd been able to take the Rooke Chapel Ringers, his own choir, to a festival he was conducting. He was really excited about showcasing his own choir in a festival, and we had worked hard on the music beforehand so that we'd set an example for the rest of the choirs. It was a very neat thing to be a part of, especially when we walked in and heard whispers of, "There's Dr. Payn's choir," or "Those are the Rooke Chapel Ringers." But with that honor also came responsibility. I know I was not the only one of us feeling the pressure to get it right.

I was excited because I'd never attended one of these festivals. They consist of multiple choirs learning a whole bunch of music together and then performing a concert at the end. These are considered "massed ringing" events, and I found it very different than playing as one choir. It was a brand-new experience of ringing with so many more bells around me. For once, other people were ringing my same part.

I was hooked immediately. Even though we were in an elementary school gymnasium whose acoustics were not the best for music, the sound was still incredible. It was about three or four more choirs than we'd had at our reunion, and it was simply massive in a particularly good way. It didn't blow out anyone's ear drums like a rock concert can, but it was still a wall of sound that took over the room. There were just so many bells!

DP was no less strict about his requirements for making music. Just because there were choirs of varying ability levels attending didn't mean he was letting anyone off the hook. We rehearsed until everyone got it right, and if there was something someone couldn't figure out, they had to ask their neighbor for help so all of the parts were clearly there, timed right, and playing at the right dynamic, whether it be loud, soft, or in-between. He even had our choir demonstrate a few times to show exactly how he wanted things done. That proved to be highly effective. After a lot of rehearsing, the pieces really came together.

One of the pieces we played that weekend was an arrangement of "The First Noel" by Cathy Moklebust. I tend to tire of Christmas music after the holidays are over, but I came to love this arrangement because of its flowing nature. It's a straightforward arrangement of the beloved carol, but if played the right way, the simple melody reveals its delicacy, full of musical detail and nuance. Dynamics and phrasing are absolutely critical. Ringing all of the notes exactly together on the beat is a challenge because many of the chords are very exposed. There is no other music going on to hide slip-ups if someone comes in a half or quarter of a beat early or late. It's also a captivating, almost mesmerizing piece that can really transport the listener to a peaceful, holiday scene, much like a Thomas Kinkade painting. To this day, it's one of my favorite pieces, no matter the time of year.

Our annual spring concert was emotional in a way it had never been before because it was DP's very last as director of the Rooke Chapel Ringers. But there were light moments too, like when we played Coldplay's "Viva la Vida," arranged by Kevin McChesney. It was so much fun to play a timely pop song, and of course we concluded our concert with "Festive Dance" as we always do.

But before we got to our finale, we interrupted DP for a special gift we had for him. To mark the occasion of DP's retirement, Christian Humcke, one of the extremely talented bell ringers who was also a music major and talented composer, wrote a song for us to perform for DP. For weeks, we snuck around practicing before and after our regularly scheduled rehearsals with DP to somehow pull off this piece. It wasn't an easy one to play, and we wanted to do it well as a surprise at our spring concert.

The piece, entitled "Jubilations," was an upbeat, dance-like piece that just sounded happy and celebratory. It was fun to play because it had a catchy melody, lots of malleting of bells, and most of all, one of our own had written it. It just sounded like it belonged, like it was written for what it was meant for, to celebrate DP's accomplishments and retirement and send him off proud and happy. Watching his reaction to us playing the piece was the most priceless part of the entire process. First, surprise crossed his face, then happiness as the surprise began to wear off. Finally, gratitude, with tears in his eyes showing us how proud he was. With his tears, of course, came our own. All of us, so proud, so honored to have played for him, so sad this was the end, tried to hold it together so we could get through our finale.

Playing that entire final concert was extremely emotional for me, knowing that he would be retiring and wouldn't be at Bucknell anymore and that we were part of his send-off. As humans, we tend to put a lot of emphasis on "lasts," and it will always be known that we were his last bell choir. I felt proud and honored to be a part of it, but also sad because it was truly the end of an era. But as DP likes to say, "This isn't goodbye, it's see you later."

Finishing that year made me realize that I didn't want to go without bells in my life again. I didn't want all of it to be over. I'd experienced what getting that passion back in my life felt like, and I was willing to do what I had to do to keep it that way. Just because I wasn't in college anymore and had kids and adult commitments didn't mean I was going to stop doing what I loved.

I was fed. I was a better person, a happier person, a person truly aligned with what I wanted to do. And that meant I was also better for everyone else. Taking time for my own enjoyment made me a better wife and mom. It also made me a great role model for my kids.

When something is your passion, you can't just let it go because you grew out of it or it's no longer convenient. If it's truly a passion, it's worth making time for even if that's difficult to do. I didn't know what that would look like going forward, but I made sure that I was open to possibilities and maintained my connections in the bell world, since DP was no longer in it full time.

I didn't know it yet, but I would get to not only do some substitute ringing but also go on tour with the Rooke Chapel Ringers two more times. Better yet, I'd play under DP's baton again after all.

6

With Our Passions Come Our People

Music is the universal language of mankind.
—Henry Wadsworth Longfellow

It was the fall of 2017 in New Bern, a quaint little town at the intersection of the Neuse and Trent rivers near the North Carolina coast. So little, in fact, that its airport had one belt for luggage and two doors leading to the tarmac. I'm quite certain it had a total of about five employees at any one time, something I would have gone my entire life without knowing if I hadn't come to North Carolina for Distinctly Bronze that year.

Three years earlier, when DP had retired, he'd told us he was scheduled to do a massed ringing event in New Bern in 2016, and it would be great if we could get a bunch of Rooke Chapel Ringer alumni to attend. We'd have a ton of fun and make up at least a small contingent of the ringers there.

A group of us applied and got in—but Hurricane Matthew hit New Bern directly in October of 2016. It would have been catastrophic for us to go ahead with our event, so it was postponed until 2017. Now here I was, at my first truly large bell festival, open only to those who applied via audition and were invited to attend. I was almost euphoric to get to do with this with DP and several other Rooke Chapel Ringers. Any event I got to be a part of with him and other alums after his retirement was a precious gift of more time and more glorious music.

When I walked into the ballroom at the convention center for our first rehearsal, I felt intimidated and overwhelmed, although I tried not to show it. Judging by the shirts from previous events many wore, it seemed the majority of the people had attended an event like this before and were seemingly seasoned at these things, but this was all new to me. I was comforted by the fact that I was one of the few people in that room who knew DP well enough that I could call him DP, and that we were close enough that I could hug him or chat with him at breaks without any formalities. I had the advantage of familiarity and history on my side. Most of these people might be seasoned festivalgoers, but I could call DP a friend.

There were people buzzing all about and a collective din of small conversations going on all over the room, punctuated by the occasional ring of a bell or the grunting movements of chairs or tables. Even in early October in North Carolina, it was warm and muggy outside, and the cool air conditioning in the room was a very welcome change. I especially appreciated the water, coffee, tea, and iced tea station, as I'm an avid iced tea drinker, my caffeine of choice. Being in the south, there was plenty of sweet tea, too. Iced tea is not seen as a must at break stations in the mid-Atlantic and Northeast. Maybe I'd found my people.

The entire half of the convention center ballroom was filled with tables and bells. I'd never seen anything like it. There was enough equipment in that room to easily supply nine full handbell choirs, the equivalent of several hundred thousand dollars. Not only that, but there was all of the extra stuff that single handbell choirs don't often have the luxury of having— huge chimes that cost thousands each that can only be played on movable stands, drum sets, additional percussion, and the lowest and biggest bells made to date, including a G1, which some choirs can only wish for because of its cost. For this event, most of the bells were on loan from other places, so we had access to great stuff. I was in awe.

I stopped at the registration area, which included a sort of mobile office and handbell repair station in one, with tables covered with office supplies, a printer, filing cabinets, toolboxes, and extra bell parts. Everything we could possibly need was there because this wasn't the Handbell Musicians of America's (HMA) first major event. After doing dozens of these events all over the country, they had this down to an exact science. Pencils? Got 'em. Hole reinforcements? Got 'em. Band-aids? Got 'em! Screw drivers for every possible size screw that could be too tight or too loose on a bell or even an extra handle in case one fell off a bell? Yup, all there. All I thought with my very Type A brain was, "Holy crap, that's a lot of stuff to remember!"

And I can't forget about the door prizes and the candy either. I had brought a few bags of candy to share with my neighbors and also in case I needed that mid-afternoon sugar rush. It was apparent I needn't have done so, but I was still happy to represent my Hershey heritage. Putting everyone's name in a box to be drawn for door prizes assured we would return to rehearsal on time, as at the beginning of each rehearsal, someone called a bunch of names. No one would want to miss their chance to win anything, including more candy. Clearly we cannot keep 130 bell ringers happy rehearsing for four days without a little (well, a lot) of sugar.

Not far from that set of tables was another set of long tables covered with items for a silent auction that would go on all weekend to raise money for HMA. Items ranged from homemade kitsch to candy and handbell-themed potholders, pins, and stationery. There were many items people had poured their heart and soul into, like beautiful quilts and other handsewn items, usually embroidered somewhere with music notes or handbells.

The most coveted items were, as always, original manuscripts donated by composers for the cause. There are many composers in the handbell world, and most write original compositions as well as arrangements of other songs. What makes these original scores so valuable to us ringers is that we come to learn the stories behind them. Some are commissioned by groups for a special purpose—in honor of someone, in memory of someone, on the occasion of an anniversary or an important date. Some are simply written because that's what composers do. It's fascinating to hear what the composer was envisioning when he or she wrote the piece, what they felt, and how the music came to them.

DP, for example, had offered up his original score of *Elegy*, a piece he wrote in the 1980s at the height of the AIDS epidemic. Having known wonderful people lost to the disease, he told me, the piece came to him within a few hours at the piano and took the audience through the anguish so many people felt at the time. In the handbell world, there's nothing more valuable than an original manuscript, usually hand-written, by a revered composer. Holding someone's original musical creation in its most raw form in yours hands is priceless, and for that reason, every manuscript, particularly DP's, goes for big bucks at these events.

One of my favorite stories and the piece it inspired is another one of DP's original works, "Heart Melodies." He completed it while I was in college, and we premiered it at Bucknell, where he told us the story of how it came to be. While dating, he and Ruth were on a business trip in Minneapolis for a food styling conference for Ruth's family's organic farm. They had some free time to tour the city while it was getting pounded by a powerful snowstorm. They had toured the Walker Galleries and were walking through the Walker Art Center's Minneapolis Sculpture Garden on a cold but crisp and clear night as the snow had stopped. There was no traffic, and the city was quiet and peaceful.

As they walked toward a café for dinner, a sweet, romantic melody kept playing in DP's head. It simply came to him as he walked with the woman he loved on a picture-perfect evening. At dinner afterward, he wrote this melody of their love story on a napkin.

Upon returning to Pennsylvania, he sat down to write it out, and one of the movements simply streamed from his pen in less than an hour. He named the work after a Langston Hughes poem, and that was the beginning of one of the most beautiful symphonies with bells I've ever heard. And knowing why and how it came to be made it that much more special. Every female ringer couldn't help but audibly say, "Awww" as he shared that story—for many of us, it was the most romantic thing we'd ever heard. Knowing how much the piece meant to him influenced the way we approached it and played it. We wanted to make sure we did our best to make him proud and communicate his feelings to the audience.

Past the silent auction was the conductor's podium where DP would spend his weekend, and, beyond that, the row of tables where I was assigned. Though the registration station and silent auction items would move later, these tables were in their permanent places for the weekend, concert ready, about two dozen six-foot tables across the ballroom with an aisle down the middle and about eight to ten of those in rows going toward the back, the last rows on risers so those bells and their players could be seen.

Every table was covered first in foam padding, then sleek, black corduroy tablecloths that brushed the ground on every side. Corduroy is the best material on which to play handbells, as it absorbs the right amount of sound when the bells are stopped or damped on it and projects the perfect amount of sound when the bells are rung or hit on it. On top, of course, were all of the bells. An entire room filled with bells. From any direction, it was a beautiful sea of shiny bronze on starkly contrasted black—the other reason for black tablecloths being to highlight the shimmer of the metal. And in the back were the biggest bells, silver aluminum, a beautiful complement to all of the brass.

The sight of so many bells was breathtaking, but also slightly intimidating. At this point, I could only imagine what they would all sound like. I was going to be one player in a sea of ringers, with many ringing more adeptly than me. I hoped I was lucky enough to play more adeptly than some others, too, but I was nervous.

Maybe, in fact, this was a good place to hide—among 130 other ringers, with seven or eight ringers playing my same part spread across the room. Then again, it was DP conducting this festival, not someone who didn't know who I was. DP could pick a wrong note out of those 130 ringers because his ear was so attuned, but more significantly, he knew my name and position and wouldn't hesitate to call me or anyone else out if we made mistakes.

Actually, not knowing someone else's name had never been a problem for DP. When someone played a wrong note, we got used to hearing iterations of, "Red shirt, right side, third row." And he was always right, so there really wasn't anywhere to hide. We all grinned on concert day when we thought we had him fooled by showing up dressed for our concert in the exact same polo shirts, but nope. The joke was on us; by then he'd learned enough names that he didn't need shirt color.

Between each row of tables was enough space for us ringers to stand and ring as well as chairs for when we had a short but glorious break to sit down. I found my place in the second row on the stage right side of the ballroom. I was playing bells A5 and B5. Everyone for about five rows directly in front of me and directly behind me was in position seven like I was, playing the same bells and parts in the music. The idea was that we would play in exact unison.

The good thing about playing with so many people on the same part is that we can always ask our forward and backward neighbors for help when we need it. We don't get that luxury when we're playing as a single choir. For example, if there was a particularly tricky part that required quick bell changes or playing more than one bell in each hand, one of us could cover one bell and the other one could cover the other one or two. That way, each note would surely be accounted for instead of each of us trying and potentially not succeeding in covering any of them. That's oftentimes what makes these performances more seamless.

This also requires a lot more communication between ringers, and the ones I had met so far all seemed friendly, welcoming, and supportive. Even though I'd felt intimidated coming into the big room, I never felt like an outsider. Bell ringers become family, and I got taken in quickly. It helped that in front of me on my same part was Beth Judd, an amazing ringer, accomplished conductor and composer, and incredibly kind person who could easily cover anything that challenged me. Whenever I felt discouraged about mastering something, she reassured me by saying, "Don't worry, honey, I've been doing this sixty years. When you've been doing it that long, you'll be able to easily do all of this." On my left, I met a lovely older woman from Texas, and on my right was another Bucknell alumna, Emily. It was comforting and so much fun to be ringing next to someone I'd rung with years prior.

With all 130 ringers in their respective spots at 2 p.m., we kicked off the first rehearsal. It was both exciting and nerve-racking. Before we even rang a single note, we did some warm-up exercises and stretches, particularly for our shoulders, neck, and hands. Neck rolling, reaching above our heads and straight out in front of us, and bending our wrists seemed a bit unnecessary to me because most handbell choirs don't need to do these things before shorter rehearsals. But since we were going to be playing for about six hours, it was pretty important that we give our arms and shoulders some love.

After the first several hours, I came to realize how important that stretching actually was. Many ringers had also brought soft, rubber mats to stand on—definitely a key takeaway for me. Standing on a concrete ballroom floor for hours at a time is not kind to your legs, no matter what shoes you're wearing. We got the occasional moment to sit down, which was also completely necessary during such a long rehearsal. Under normal circumstances, when a weekly rehearsal is more like a couple of hours, there are no chairs there to drop into for a quick break.

When we were finally ready to begin playing our bells, I took a deep breath. We were starting at the beginning of the program with a fairly straightforward piece whose quick tempo would grab the audience immediately. It was made up of many flowing sixteenth notes in a melodic line meant to sound completely seamless, just as if it was played on a carillon. Aptly, it was entitled "Carillon" (by H. Dean Wagner).

Usually found in a bell tower, a carillon is a set of twenty-three bells played by one person operating a keyboard with her fists and pedals with her feet, which makes it sound smooth and harmonious. The challenge of this first piece would be getting 130 of us to ring together in that same coherent way, which would require not only connection with the conductor, DP, but connection between all of us. This was also one of the easier pieces in the repertoire and a way for DP to gauge where the group was—would we connect and gel together immediately? Had we all practiced at home like we were supposed to? Were we all as intimately familiar with the music as we should have been for being selected to such a distinguished group? Time would tell.

The first time through that piece was a blur, but it was a good blur. We began with the piece under tempo and worked our way up as the days went on. The first time through, I exhaled a huge breath at the end. Yes, I had made a couple of errors, but I was seemingly unscathed. I was impressed with myself.

I was even more impressed with the entire room. The sound that came out of those bells and swelled all around us was huge.

It filled that half-ballroom and spilled out into the hallways and even the bathrooms. All at once, nine choirs of bells were sounding out as one great, glorious choir. Of course it was the first piece of the first rehearsal, so there was a ways to go, but I'll never forget hearing us for the first time. It was just so *much* sound, in a good way. Honestly, my mind was blown. This was way more than a band or orchestra, so much different than any other ensemble I had ever been in. Immense, and yet connected. Maybe that was the best way to describe it.

Over the course of the next few days, we rehearsed and rehearsed and rehearsed some more. We rehearsed in sectionals—upper bells only and lower bells only at separate times—and then back together as one. It became clear which pieces were going to need the most work and which ones were more for fun. It's so important to include both, not only for the audience but also for the ringers.

One of the most popular with both the ringers and the audience was DP's arrangement of "Suite for Downton Abbey," complete with servant's bell at the appropriate places. Definitely a fan favorite, but not an easy piece. Its popularity at the time, however, gave the group the push it needed to perfect it.

These rehearsals went long, and there were times when I wanted nothing more than to sit down or even grab a ten-minute nap under one of those long tablecloths—I didn't even mind if rehearsing went on around me. My feet started to ache, and near the end of those marathon rehearsals, the notes began to swim on the pages. Thank goodness for the candy and iced tea. The sugar and caffeine got me through until the next break or meal.

The most captivating thing about those rehearsals was the progress—so much in four short days. We had come together as a group for the first time on Thursday afternoon, having worked independently on each of our parts in areas all around the country. By Sunday afternoon, we were ready for a concert.

One of the pieces that stood out as a barometer of how far we'd come was Toccata, from the organ suite *Gothique* by Leon Boellmann and arranged by Matthew Compton. As its name implies, this was a piece from an organ suite, meaning it was originally written for organ, an instrument that not only has a keyboard to operate it, but also pedals and stops and pipes. In other words, a huge, complicated instrument that requires someone specially trained to play it well. This piece was written to mimic that instrument, with many moving parts in mind, the melody moving from bass to treble and back again. In fact, there were so many notes simply written on the physical music for the piece that it would easily give anyone black note anxiety—an expression in music that means feeling intimidated by seeing lots of notes to be played in a small space. It's scary.

Not only were there a lot of notes, but this piece had a tempo or speed suggestion that seemed simply ludicrous. There was more than one time when we looked at that tempo and collectively laughed because there was no way in hell we would ever pull that off. In fact, there was actually physically no way to play all of those notes and count them at the same time—some of us would literally just be ringing our bells as many times as possible in a row without counting to create this music, something we rarely get to do as musicians.

Though we ringers were convinced it was never going to happen, DP operated as if it was a forgone conclusion, exuding all the confidence in the world. He was determined to get us to play that piece at the suggested tempo despite all of our grumblings, of which there were many. We started at a slow tempo on Thursday, working again and again to get all of the right notes at the right times, and by Friday we were on our way to increasing the tempo.

Have you ever done something so incrementally, maybe hastening your walking or jogging pace for example, that you don't even realize you've done it until you're going practically twice the speed at which you began? Well, that's exactly what we did. DP took the metronome and kept checking it as we'd rehearse, and then he'd click it up one more notch. Just one more notch at a time. Slowly, very slowly, we were getting faster. When we'd have a hiccup, we'd stop and work it out, counting slowly, adjusting who was playing which bells, even splitting parts among all of us. But we kept working at it one click at a time until we were just about there. By the time we were just about where we wanted it, we knew we had increased our tempo dramatically. We'd done it!

When I listen to the recording of us performing that piece, I still can't believe how far we got in four days' time. It was a stellar example of what can be done with lots and lots of patience and perseverance, no matter what it is—music, training to win a race, perfecting a skill.

We were able to perfect and perform that piece not only because we were adept, high-level ringers but also because we knew how important our connection was to each other and to DP. We relied on him to lead us, guide us, and help us achieve that tempo increase. We relied on our neighbors to play their parts, coming in at the right times with the right notes so that our parts fit together perfectly. When a group like that plays together for that amount of time, each person gets to know what their neighbor is doing and when, how to move and flow with each other, and how to truly become one instrument.

As Jenny Cauhorn, previous executive director of the Handbell Musicians of America explains it, "Handbells are like a living keyboard. The ringers have to connect to each other on a totally different level than in another ensemble. It truly takes each ringer to perform at the same level to accomplish the excellence we strive for. Everyone is equal and equally necessary because if you miss a note, it's a big deal."

This was even more true of other pieces we performed that were more lyrical and musical, requiring subtle nuances and phrasing. These were the pieces in which we had to concentrate fully on watching DP conduct, memorizing our parts so we could look up and play together, to the point that we even breathed together. One hundred thirty-seven people, eyes on one man, breathing at the same time, mimicking his motions and emotions so the notes would fall into place and we could become the music for the audience.

For me, this is where the real music happens. It's in the details, the way we connect to each other, the way we anticipate each other's movements and mimic the way each other plays. When there is so much nuance that the music completely gels together, it truly becomes a group experience. Everyone feels it, even though everyone may experience it differently. It's like a special bond only the group has and that nobody else experiences, even if they hear the music. It's a connection between the musicians and the notes, the musicians and each other, and musicians and the conductor.

I'll never forget rehearsing one piece and just nailing it. It was so incredibly beautiful that we had all stunned ourselves, when DP said, "And that was musical orgasm." Like my neighbor to my left, there were quite a few older southern ladies in our midst, so there was a lot of blushing and giggling going on, but there really wasn't a better description. When we followed that by an equally stunning few measures, he then exclaimed, "And that was the cigarette!"

One of these more lyrical and more meaningful pieces—because we knew the story behind it—was also one of DP's original compositions. It was entitled "Transitions," and it was written for a Bucknell student whose parents had commissioned DP to write it for his graduation. I never even thought of such a thing despite the fact that composers write commissions in honor of people all of the time. I knew that DP poured his heart and soul into his compositions, so I imagined the time, effort, creativity, and thought that went into this. I thought it was one of the most heartfelt gifts anyone could ever receive.

"Transitions" was about just that: this student's transition from a young, inexperienced but excited freshman to a senior in college, a grown man who was headed for great things. I had not been a part of the group during his time, but I felt the emotions nonetheless. At the beginning of the piece, I felt the hope, the newness of the college adventure, and the excitement for what was to come. I could hear the promise of new days and new adventures and the anticipation that most college kids have. Throughout the piece, I felt the moments of growth, of struggle, of worry about the unknown. There are notes of melancholy and anxiety, even sadness, expressing the emotions all of us have gone through over the course of four years, particularly those attending college and experiencing the inordinate amount of growth that happens there.

As the piece came to close, I felt the sense of accomplishment, relief, and pride. I didn't need to be that student to know what was going on in DP's mind as he wrote that piece, and I didn't need to be that student for it to move me to tears. That piece still moves me to tears. It's just a plainly beautiful work that tells a story so clearly. I can put myself right into that work, walking through campus, feeling the emotions it portrays. The fact that it's tied to Bucknell makes it that much more special, especially for each of us Rooke Chapel Ringers. We played it so well too. I felt a huge emotional release when we were finished.

It might seem difficult to express these emotions in a concert without words or gestures, but we still get our message through with the way we play our bells. Our body and arm movements, our eyes, and our faces convey how we're feeling. How we watch the conductor and make eye contact with audience members demonstrate the emotions of a piece. In fact, it's rarely a problem to express our feelings with our bells, but rather more of a challenge to keep a straight face when something hasn't gone right. The audience often doesn't recognize a mistake, and if they do, they usually don't know where it came from. The only thing that outs us as players is if we make a scrunched, I-made-a-mistake face in the middle of a piece. Emoting with bells is easy; not giving away our mistakes when we make them is hard.

We worked that weekend to prepare and perfect an entire concert's worth of music, including lots of other gorgeous and fun pieces. The most fun of them was probably Michael Jackson's "Thriller" arranged by Nick Hanson, the director of Handbell Ensembles at the Potomac School in McLean, Virginia. Hanson has made a name for himself in the handbell world with his arrangements of popular songs, from Broadway classics like "All That Jazz" to songs by Adele, Elton John, and even the theme from *Game of Thrones*. This has kept his fifth-through twelfth-grade students engaged, and it has enlivened the handbell world with new ways to relate to audiences.

"Thriller" was our finale, and it was a huge crowd pleaser. And the audience got a surprise when DP walked out to the podium fully dressed as Michael Jackson from the "Thriller" music video, costumed head to toe in red and black leather complete with wig. The audience went wild for it. Many of the ringers were surprised, too, with the exception of anyone who had been at a festival with DP previously and the small group of us who were in on the brief moon-walking lesson the night before.

When several Rooke Chapel Ringer alumni and friends had gathered at the bed and breakfast where DP and Ruth were staying, most of us learned for the first time of his penchant for dressing up for the finale numbers at these festivals. He let the cat out of the bag that this time he had a costume but still needed to master the moonwalk. We all laughed until we cried as we watched one of our alums teach DP to moonwalk. It was both fascinating and endearing for us to watch DP, master of so many things, attempting to tackle something new. We were all giving him pointers, none of which helped, and we all chuckled, especially Ruth, as he looked clumsy and almost took a couple spills. It felt so good to see someone we admire so much be in the same position that we are often in with him—learning something new, making mistakes, being vulnerable, and needing encouragement.

Fun was the theme of the weekend for me. The first night we were there, we went out for drinks after rehearsal, just the Rooke Chapel Ringer alumni who were in attendance and DP, to reminisce, laugh, and relive old stories. We were already a family of our own, even though we'd never all played in the same choir at the same time.

We knew that we didn't want this to be the last time we gathered this way. To that end, Jenny Cauhorn of HMA announced that the Rooke Chapel Ringers should form an alumni choir to take to HMA's National Seminar coming up in Michigan that following July. Of course we were absolutely tickled at the possibility—our enthusiasm was palpable and contagious, and I knew it wasn't just the wine talking.

DP was not so sure about this plan. In fact, I swear I saw a passing look of terror on his face. Knowing it would be a lot of work and pressure for him and secretly thinking we would never be able to pull it off, he gave us a challenge. He told us that if we could find enough Rooke Chapel Ringer alumni to form two choirs to perform, he would make it happen. He wanted at least twenty-eight alumni so that we could cover and help each other, especially in a group of ringers who had never all played together before and would be coming from different ringing situations since leaving Bucknell. I knew he didn't have much confidence that there would be twenty-eight alums who would give up their vacation time, family time, or extra cash to gather for four days in Michigan in the middle of the summer.

Oh, how he underestimated a few Type A alumni and the Rooke Chapel Ringers! Much to his chagrin, we had at least fifteen ringers commit within the first hour of coming up with this idea, and we knew with a few call outs, Facebook posts, and emails, we could easily find another thirteen. From that moment, it was on. We, two other alums and myself in particular, were full steam ahead on getting the Rooke Chapel Ringer alumni choir to Michigan. DP just rolled his eyes and ordered another glass of wine. I'm pretty sure he prayed pretty hard that night that it wouldn't happen.

That very next summer, we were waiting to perform for the Handbell Musicians of America National Seminar in Grand Rapids, Michigan. I looked around at us assembled backstage, all dressed in variations of performance black in stark contrast to the white cinderblock walls that snaked around us like a maze. This group of Rooke Chapel Ringer alumni was remarkable. From graduating years 1988–2020, including an incoming freshman and his alumnus father and some honorary alums who did us a huge favor by ringing with us at the last minute, we were a force to be reckoned with. Not only a handbell force, but an amazing, everyday walk of life force. All of us had come together from all over the country, reuniting for this one special purpose: an alumni concert at National Seminar.

It was inspiring. People had taken vacation from work, traveled by plane or hours by car, booked hotel rooms or Airbnbs, and spent significant amounts of money, all to come together and play one more time. We had never actually played together as this particular group, but almost all of us had played as Rooke Chapel Ringers under DP's baton. When the opportunity for so many of us to perform together came, twenty-four of us had ended up jumping at the chance.

We'd gathered just two days before in a hot, small rehearsal room late on a Tuesday afternoon. We had all of Tuesday afternoon and evening, all day Wednesday, and a couple short hours Thursday morning to put together a forty-minute program that would knock the socks off our audience—because that's what the Rooke Chapel Ringers do. DP had made it absolutely clear that if we had gotten enough of us together to make this happen, each of us needed to practice our parts at home and come completely prepared.

We didn't disappoint him. Everyone came more prepared than he'd expected, with parts worked on and kinks worked out, and within the first few minutes in that cramped, sweaty room, we were making music. There were some stops and starts at first, some back and forth on tempo and who was covering which bells, particularly in the bass section. After all, many of us had spent years playing after Bucknell and had gotten used to certain patterns and ways of doing things that might have to be temporarily broken. There was also much chatter in the room as old friends reunited and new friendships were made.

And what's a reunion without inside jokes? We wickedly made fun of DP's waning eyesight, although he certainly wasn't the only one who'd aged. In typical Rooke Chapel Ringer (RCR) fashion, there were at least three times when we started to rehearse something at measure 69 in some piece. For most people, that means nothing. For us, it always drew giggles and snickers because no one in our group could ever say "69" without connoting a sexual reference. That's how we knew we were us.

The music came together quickly. And not just playing the music on the page, but assimilating all of DP's directions, breathing with him, and making moving, beautiful artistry. I'll never forget the moment, about an hour into that first rehearsal, when we played something and DP exclaimed, "There it is. That's my choir!" The relief and pride in his voice, the collective smile of the group, was a joy that couldn't be contained in our little rehearsal. We were happy to be together, excited to be doing this thing we loved so much, and so thrilled to be able to do it with and for DP.

Now we were standing behind the stage with the A/C blasting us until we had goosebumps though most of our palms were sweating. There was just a single door separating us from the audience. I was more nervous than I expected. Perhaps nervous wasn't really it—I was excited, but also somewhat melancholy. I was thrilled to have the opportunity to play with these amazing musicians, for this man we all revered and would clearly travel hundreds of miles for. I was eager to play, but also eager to savor the moment. I knew there would never be another one like it. This particular group would never play together again, and this could very well be the last time I would play for DP. That weighed on my heart.

Before I knew it, the door swung open and out we went into a grand ballroom, much larger than the one I played in in North Carolina, with rows and rows of chairs as far as any of us could see, the exit signs appearing tiny at the back from our vantage point. The majority of the chairs were full—we were surprised at the number of people in attendance for a lunchtime concert.

And these were our people. These were the best of the best, the bell geeks, the bell groupies, the one audience who would understand exactly what we were trying to accomplish. They would get every nuance, appreciate every phrase, and know all of the inside jokes. These were DP's colleagues and cohorts and superfans. We weren't doing a great job just for us, we were doing it for him.

As I listened to Jenny Cauhorn introduce us, I became once again acutely aware of how special this was. She said that she and DP had been hoping to make this happen for years—bringing his choir to showcase at Seminar—and now it had happened. And it had happened with alumni on top of that, former RCRs sacrificing time and money to join together in Michigan and play this concert. She told the audience we'd had exactly two days to prepare this music, and that we were ready.

I stood in my position, D5/E5, with my arms at my sides, hands linked behind my back as DP had taught us to do. He always reminded us that the special stuff was in the details—how we stood, how we moved, how we carried ourselves. He was always right. The details are what separate excellent from good, no matter what you're doing. I looked out into that dark sea of people and felt not only the bright, hot lights on us but also the pressure of it all, knowing it was also being live-streamed all over the world and into my own family room where my husband, kids, and in-laws were watching. My heart was beating out of my chest, my palms were slippery as I tried to dry them on my dress, because in true Rooke Chapel Ringer fashion, we do not wear gloves. I knew I was taking shallow, quick breaths because I was so nervous and excited simultaneously, and yet I tried to remind myself that the most important thing to do was to enjoy it.

Suddenly, DP was in front of us, and it was go time. We collectively smiled because that's not just what he taught us to do but also just what we did when we saw him on the podium—smiled at this man we wanted to perform so well for. He had timed every piece and every word he was going to say to the second because we were told we had exactly forty minutes and no more. As he picked up his hands, we put ours on our bells, many of us trying stealthily to make sure we had the right ones even though we had checked and double-checked while we were being introduced. And when he lifted his arms, we brought our bells up to our shoulders, the ready position for making music. As he breathed in with his preparatory beat, we did as well, getting ready to ring that very first note.

And it was glorious. The sound filled the ballroom, and we were once again the Rooke Chapel Ringers. The gorgeous music we created was just that—gorgeous and melodious and precise. We watched intently, letting the tiny bit of muscle memory we had started to build take over so that we could focus on the musicality, the connection we had with him. Our musical phrases ebbed and flowed with the movement of his arms, our dynamics mimicking the size of his gestures. From the first row where I was standing, I could see the rest of the first choir to my right and left, and everyone was smiling. I tried to watch these other incredible musicians as I maintained my own part, in awe of what we could accomplish in just two days. I couldn't see our second choir behind us, but I could clearly hear how well they were playing.

DP had carefully selected our repertoire for that concert, including his own "Transitions" because the student it was written for was playing with us, a piece entitled "Time and Tide" written by alumnus Rob Riker, who was also playing with us, and several others. "Transitions" still meant so much to me, but there were two other pieces that I also thoroughly loved. The first one, called "Spires" and written by Matthew Compton, was and remains captivating. Matt was also playing in the group with us because we did, at the last minute, need a few "ringer" ringers to fill some holes in the second choir, and he shared with us the visions he had when writing the piece.

Dr. Payn conducting the Rooke Chapel Ringer Alumni Choir
in Grand Rapids, photo courtesy J.R. Smith

He told us he wrote it as he was thinking about the great mountainous spires of the Cascades near his home in Portland, Oregon. He had imagined how they came into being, from the beginning of the earth forming, to the mountain ranges clashing together, to how life subsequently began to form. The piece begins quietly and ends quietly with walls of sound throughout, simulating the moving of the earth and the formation of these magnificent peaks, rising up from the ground below and reaching into the sky. The way the piece begins and ends with big chords made it absolutely imperative that we played precisely, watching DP as he directed each individual strike of the clapper on our bells, so we played exactly in unison. Between those glorious chords, flowing, cascading notes all the way down the scale were reminiscent of a waterfall and the slow, gentle coming to life of the forest flora and fauna. We nailed that piece, with both accuracy and musicality, and at the end, you could have heard a pin drop in the room. DP acknowledged Matt, and we all clapped loudly for his composing ability.

Our second to last piece was an unpublished piece written by Arnold Sherman entitled "Variations on an Old Nursery Rhyme." It was the quintessential moment of silliness and fun in a concert for a bunch of bell groupies. It was written tongue in cheek, in the style of multiple well-known bell composers. The "old nursery rhyme" was "Three Blind Mice," and the composer had taken the time to write variations of the rhyme in the style of several different composers.

It was particularly appropriate for this group because almost everyone in the audience recognized each composer within the first few notes of his or her section, including DP's, which echoed the style of some of his most popular pieces and his signature running eighth notes that often led into triplets. There was a section for Kevin McChesney, who had transcribed our signature "Festive Dance" with so much of his section being malleted, as that's his style. Each time a new composer was introduced, the audience laughed, recognizing who was being featured or made fun of, depending on how we looked at it. It was a great way to interact with the audience, us having as much fun as they were, especially since some of those composers were in attendance.

We wouldn't have been the Rooke Chapel Ringers if we didn't finish the program with our signature piece, "Festive Dance," as only we could perform it—always wanting to go faster, pushing and pushing the tempo until we're almost on the edge of a total train wreck. But we have so much fun when we're ringing it, and the audience loves it just as much. As had become a new tradition, several ringers tossed Beanie Baby flamingoes around, the bass bell ringers hoping to catch each of them in a bass bell as we held our last note. In familiar form, DP then looked at his watch, pretending to see just how long he could leave us ringing that note. And when he cut that final note off in a flourish, the audience was immediately on its feet.

That forty minutes passed more quickly than any other forty-minute period of my life. The standing ovation by the entire audience was emotional even for the least emotive person there, given that the audience now knew what it took for us to get there and that a goal of DP's had been fulfilled. DP turned around and looked at us, each one, and mouthed, "Thank you," blowing each of us a kiss as he always did when he was pleased. He then took the time to shake each one of our hands or give us a big hug as the audience continued to applaud.

I knew he was proud and happy with what we'd done. And we were happy with what we'd done. Though there might have been small snafus, there is no such thing as a perfect performance. We all knew we'd done our best. We hugged each other, thrilled for the opportunity we'd had and loving having been together.

7

Too Much
or Too Little?

You often feel tired,
not because you've done too much,
but because you've done too little
of what sparks a light in you.
—Alexander den Heijer

My passion for handbells lights me up. I smile bigger when I'm talking about handbells or hanging out with other ringers. I laugh more, and I enjoy what I'm doing. When I pick up those bells to ring them, I feel comforted and excited at the same time. I love the way they feel, the handle smooth in my palms, the weight of the bells resting in my hands. I love the movements I make to ring the bells, the way my arms flow around and around and the way I flick my wrist to make the clapper hit the bell, all while always slightly moving my feet, never standing perfectly still.

I love reading the music and finding something I hadn't found before, mastering a measure that's challenging me, and simply using the part of my brain that allows me to comprehend and translate that information into musical notes. Making that music fills me up so much that no matter how tired I might be at the time, and sometimes that is pretty damn tired, I still enjoy it.

I was reminded of the way ringing can be both invigorating and exhausting in February of 2019, when I had the privilege of ringing at another Distinctly Bronze event, this time on the West Coast. DP was again the conductor and clinician, assisted by conductor and composer Brian Childers. I couldn't have been more grateful to have the chance to ring under DP's direction once more. Neither of us is getting any younger.

The event was held in Portland, Oregon—the farthest I'd ever traveled away from my children. And in my mind, going across the country was a big step in my parenting journey. I was way too far away if anything happened, and the three-hour time difference was a challenge for communication as well as for my six-year-old to understand.

DP and I flew to Portland together. We've learned that we're quite compatible travel partners, especially when it came to pre-flight wine, which was a must-have. Lucky for me, he's also easy to keep track of, given that he has at least one foot on my five-foot, two-inch frame. Most airplane seats aren't very accommodating of his long legs, but in this case a kind man switched seats with him so that he could have the aisle next to me rather than the middle seat behind me he had been assigned.

We had some good laughs when DP needed me to read his tab or make sure he had his phone and his wallet. His wife Ruth had tasked me with keeping track of him since she wasn't there to keep him in line herself. She and I have a running joke that at least one of us has to be there to make sure he gets everywhere he needs to go with everything he needs. Though DP is a brilliant musician and endearing person, people are sometimes surprised to know that he can be just as human and forgetful as the rest of us.

It's in those moments of shared humanity that I enjoy his company the most. Whether we were bitching and moaning about the security line or really starting to get weary as we got to Seattle with yet another flight to go, I feel privileged that I don't just get to drop into his professional life every now and then but have made a true friend who can share the mundane and asinine parts of life. Traveling together that day was the longest stretch of time he and I had ever had to be together and talk, and it was a gift, I hope, for both of us.

Ruth and I also tag-team on these trips to make sure none of DP's admirers get too friendly. We've laughed for years at the women who practically throw themselves at him, never caring that he's married. So I also get to play the role of loving, temporarily adopted, and very protective daughter. Not only does it help keep his female fan club away, but, as we joke, it helps keep the celebrity from going to his head. When we start to see him get his ego stroked a bit too much, one of us always reminds him who he is. More than once I've reminded him he's just like the rest of us by saying, "Ok, smart guy, don't get too cocky—remember, you lost your wallet on your last trip," or "You talk a big talk, but you can't see that music without your glasses, so don't forget them."

Since DP and I are East Coasters, the entire day Wednesday was a travel day, and we began rehearsing on Thursday afternoon. By 5 p.m. Thursday, all of that caught up with me as I was taking breaks by lying in a fetal position in the corner of the ballroom. I have this great ability to be able to nap anywhere, and that served me well on this trip because that time difference hit hard. I think I was finally just about adjusted by the time it was time to leave on Monday. Fighting through that time change fatigue as well as three and a half solid days of ringing bells was tough.

At the same time, I had the time of my life. Since this was my second Distinctly Bronze event, walking into the ballroom felt like coming home. Seeing familiar faces, including some awesome Bucknell alumni, was like reuniting with family. Between my previous Distinctly Bronze event in North Carolina and National Seminar in Michigan, I knew so many more people. It was so comforting and welcoming to look around and ring among people who'd become friends.

In my new position on higher bells, I had a friend from Japan on my left, a friend from Maryland on my right, and a friend from Ohio in front of me, all of whom I had met in Michigan. Having those people there made it so much more fun to ring, and being able to look to your neighbor for support is key when playing bells. Not only was I ringing with these people every day, but I was also housing with ten of them, which forced us to get to know each other very quickly. There were three people in our bedroom, we shared a bathroom with another two people, and we shared a kitchen, family room, groceries, everything—just like a family.

I was also excited about playing E6/F6, a position that required me to ring with two bells in each hand at multiple times, or, in bell speak, four-in-hand ringing. This was thrilling for me because it's a skillset I'd been wanting to work on for a long time. Instead of just having four bells in front of me most of the time, I had at least eight. Sometimes I had to pick up only two, one in each hand. Sometimes I had to pick up two in one hand and one in the other. Sometimes I needed two bells in each hand, and in order to do that, I had to properly position them on the table before we even started playing. I had to make sure they were turned in the right direction so I'd pick them up the right way, or else the bells wouldn't ring when they're supposed to.

In addition to all of the bells on the table, we also have extra things like mallets, handchimes, wooden sticks, and even extra percussion (this concert even required kazoos). All of this makes for a very chaotic looking tabletop, although each ringer must be aware at all times of what's where and whether it's in the right place. Grabbing something in the wrong spot at the wrong time or in the wrong way can become catastrophic when there's little time to fix a mistake. That could mean wrong notes, missing notes, or even air rings in which we make the motion to ring the bell, but it doesn't ring. That still surprises even the most seasoned of us ringers, and it's one of those mistakes we have to cover up by not making a funny face in the middle of concert if and when it happens.

The ballroom itself was welcomingly different than the one in North Carolina. Its walls of windows on two sides looked right out into the huge, snow-covered pine trees of the Northwest. The refreshing natural light streaming into that room was invigorating, especially after so much time on airplanes and so much focus on the black and white pages of our music. I felt like the trees were a living audience to our rehearsals, sort of holding us up, encouraging us and giving us the energy to keep improving. I felt like they were towering silent cheerleaders for us, waiting to welcome an audience into the room to witness what they'd been privy to for three days.

We had about 100 people at that event, making up seven to eight choirs of ringers. The difficulty of the repertoire, the ability of the ringers, and the availability of bells determine the lowest bells that are used for each event, and for this event, we had everything down to a C2, which would be the equivalent of the second C note on the way up a piano from the bottom. It wasn't quite as many bells and didn't go as low as we had in North Carolina, but nonetheless, a ballroom filled with gorgeous bells in beautiful surroundings was impressive as always.

DP had chosen a varied and fun repertoire for our concert, including pieces like "I Got Rhythm," "Eleanor Rigby," and *The Muppet Show* theme song. We had a lot of laughs working on those as well as a hoe-down piece that really underwent a stellar transformation in the almost four days we rehearsed it. Brian Childers, our associate conductor, wrote "Ole' Dan Tucker Hoedown" and conducted it for us. It sticks in my memory both because it was such an interesting transition as we learned the piece and also because my youngest daughter gets incredibly annoyed when I play it in the car (I get such joy out of torturing her with it). It wasn't a challenging piece technically, but it's a piece that requires a certain level of levity, and at the beginning of the process, we were all playing so straight and seriously. I mean, we were taking those notes on the page super seriously without any regard to the title of the song, which does in fact, imply something fun.

Poor Brian stood up on that podium each time we worked on the piece and kept trying to get us to loosen up. The first two days, his attempts were futile. No one was buying into this "have fun with it" thing. Everyone was more interested in being accurate with their notes and not letting loose, which is not uncommon for us bell ringers. We're trained to be serious at these events, knowing that they are audition-only and that a certain level of expertise is expected of us. There's often an extra sense of seriousness when DP is conducting because of how well the ringers want to perform for him. However, along about day three, Brian had just had enough. He finally said, "Guys, this is a *hoedown*. It's supposed to be fun!"

He followed that with multiple sets of directions for what we were going to do to make it fun. The first was just some clapping. Okay, everyone clapped but not very loosely—we were still acting all buttoned up. The second set included some stomping and singing, and as Brian mentioned, the words were meaningless, but that was the point of the song. We had to sing females first, then males, then together.

If you aren't familiar with handbell ringers and singing, suffice it to say that most of us don't. That's why we ring, because many of us don't have the angelic voices we want to share with others. There is always an audible moan from a handbell choir when a conductor tells the ringers they have to sing.

But Brian pushed on, put in the singing, and people started, and I really mean just started, to let go a little. He kept encouraging everyone to relax, but that was a tough transition from the other pieces we were doing. So to make it even more fun, he added in some dancing because, of course, it's a hoedown. So now we were clapping, stomping, singing, and dancing.

It was at that point that the veil of seriousness was finally lifted. I mean, how could we not feel like loosening up when we were dancing around? And then Brian added that we should be hooting and hollering and yee-hawing whenever we could fit it in. Well, now there was no chance of not participating or trying to hide, so we all gave in, and man, was it fun. We couldn't play the piece without smiling because we were having so much fun and because we knew it would be a crowd pleaser. Have you ever tried to yee-haw with a frown? I don't think it's even possible.

The crowd did love it, and it's one of my favorites to listen to because I think of this transition every time—how we began so seriously and were able to really let go and instead, have such a great time. This song (among a ton of other bell recordings) is in my playlist, and every time my kids hear it, they roll their eyes, but I know secretly that they can't help but have fun too.

Of course not everything was fun and games. We played some pretty tough, serious pieces that required a great deal of rehearsal both in sectionals and as an entire group. One piece in particular, Nocturne no. 3 "Liebestraum," arranged by John Muschick, is a gorgeous, well-known work by Franz Liszt. The title means love dream, and it was the most lyrical and challenging for the group. It was throughout this piece that I found myself really relating to DP as a teacher and how he was trying to communicate what he wanted the group to do with this piece.

This was a technically difficult piece, and musicality and nuances of dynamics were incredibly important. A lot of ringers were having trouble counting and making the sixteenth notes seamless, so I began to watch DP's techniques of working through the challenges. I admired his patience as we went at these same passages again and again, seemingly making no progress. It was then that it began to get very philosophical and a little comical. DP was using analogies to really get across the idea of how beautiful this piece was supposed to sound, giving us visuals to try to get us to feel the music.

"Imagine you're hang gliding over the Grand Canyon," he ventured. "Feel the way the wind carries you, flowing freely. You're not trying to control the glider. You're letting it carry you. Let the notes flow. Don't try so hard to control each note, but feel how they connect to each other."

And everyone tried, truly. Poor DP listened each time, trying hard not to reveal a look of defeat on his face or give away too much frustration in his voice. Multiple times I watched as he took his right hand, put it on his forehead and rubbed it down the back of his head through his white ponytail, trying hard to find a way to relate to us how he wanted it to sound. A few minutes later, I heard, "Imagine you're floating through space…"

Those of us who knew DP well and who'd figured out what he was going for, stifled our giggles as we exchanged eye rolls with each other. Some ringers were just lost and not going to get it no matter how he tried to explain it. He finally gave up, knowing we'd made as much progress as we could. We didn't play that piece our absolute best for the concert, but I choose to believe that each one of us grew as musicians, nonetheless. And although I know it was frustrating for DP, I learned so much about patience and technique and persistence as a teacher and conductor.

Just as he had done at Distinctly Bronze in North Carolina, DP chose to end our concert with a song that would lend itself to a chance for him to wear a costume. It was such a thrill to learn and play "Sergeant Pepper's Lonely Hearts Club Band," which DP had specially commissioned composer Nicholas Hanson to write just for this event. I'm a Beatles fan, but for the majority of the ringers who were much more familiar with the film and got to experience the height of the Beatles stardom, it

107

was that much more fun. This one quickly became a favorite earworm of mine.

After our penultimate piece, DP disappeared. A few measures into "Sergeant Pepper," he reappeared, fully dressed as Ringo Star from the album cover, and the audience got a huge kick out of that. Head to toe in bright fuchsia pink and gold, he got lots of laughs and applause, which of course made us smile as we were ringing. It's a pretty cool tradition to end these mass ringing concerts with a conductor in costume. It reminds us that in the end, it's about the fun we're having.

Dr. Payn and me, happily accomplished after the concert
in Portland, Oregon, February 2019

That four days of ringing, despite how terribly exhausting it was, was another highlight of my handbell experience. Being in a room with that many musicians working together to achieve something is magical enough, but as handbell ringers, it's so much more. It's being in a room of friends who become family. It's being so connected to each other that you breathe together, place your notes exactly together at the right time, and anticipate each other's movements. It's loads and loads of nonverbal communication between the ringers, the ringers and conductor, and the entire ensemble and the audience. It's inside jokes and silliness and fun and lots of candy and caffeine. It's curling up in the corner for a ten-minute nap and standing on rubber padding, so our feet don't hurt. It's constant earworms when we're not in rehearsal—at meals, when going to bed, and when waking up. It's serious rehearsing and working the brain. And it takes serious time.

And that's the thing. Handbells take a lot of time. For a ringer to participate in an event like this, first comes auditioning and applying. If you're accepted, you find out what bells you've been assigned and learn the music before rehearsal even takes place. Then, the rehearsals begin in earnest for hours at a time. Preparing for one concert can easily take over 30 hours of music review and rehearsals, and that's a conservative estimate. For these events, there's often substantial travel involved, requiring flights and cars and luggage and security.

For a season of ringing in one handbell choir, the choir puts in untold rehearsal hours over the course of months. Next is the scheduling of concerts and hauling equipment, usually in a U-Haul type van given the amount and size of all of the bells, the tables, the foam, the tablecloths, and the accessories. Even local concerts require time spent in the car or carpooling, finding the right spots, and then after unloading all of the equipment, spending the first thirty minutes at a concert venue playing Tetris to figure out how we are possibly going to set up all of our equipment in a space quite different (and usually smaller) than where we rehearse. The equipment itself takes almost an hour to unload, arrange, set up, and get ready. On a tour, we easily get that sequence down to a science and cut the time by at least twenty minutes, but that's with every single ringer and the conductor pitching in. When everything is finally set up, the warm-ups and rehearsing can begin.

Oh, and don't forget the eating! No bell choir can perform a concert on empty stomachs, so there is a meal involved, whether we bring it ourselves or it's provided by the venue.

Performing is the least time-consuming of all the associated activities. In less than two hours, the concert is over, and it's time to reverse the entire process. On a day with good weather and a concert close by, the process from leaving for a concert to getting back home could take as little as five hours, but when there's travel involved, you can easily count on eight or more.

So why do we do it? For the same reasons anyone does something they feel passionately about. We love it. It feeds us. It fills us in ways nothing else does. For me, playing stretches and nurtures my brain. It challenges me in a way that's different from every other area of my life. It makes my heart happy, and it makes my soul sing.

I believe all of us need these things, these passions that light us up and make us feel alive. I believe they are integral to our happiness and fulfillment. Can you think of something that makes you feel that way? Something you'd do all the time, if you could? Are you smiling right now? Then you get what I'm saying.

The challenge is, of course, that our passions require our time, as well as planning and scheduling and maybe even babysitters or travel. They might mean early morning alarms in the dark of winter or staying up way past our bedtimes. They might mean skipping lunch breaks or forgoing tasty coffee drinks to save some money. They might even mean spending less time with our partners, spouses, children, families, friends. I've cut short some vacations to my beloved New Jersey shore and given up time with my girls and my husband.

Should we make these sacrifices for our passions? I say an adamant yes. Whether it's running marathons, creating art, writing, playing music, rock climbing, collecting stamps, or any other activity that brings us joy, these are the things that feed our souls. And our souls need to be fed, so that we can go on doing what we need and want to for others as providers, caretakers, and responsible adults. We've all heard the analogy of trying to pour from an empty bucket. We cannot continually pour from our own buckets, giving constantly to other people or other things, without refilling them.

My story sounds linear, like I leapt from one joyful handbell ringing opportunity to the next, but there were sometimes big gaps in between. And during those gaps, I sometimes felt like I had—or should—set ringing aside. I changed my mind about that after working with a very skilled life coach who had me do some soul-searching. When we whittled everything in my life down to the bare bones of who I was and wanted to be, one of the ways I described myself was as a musician—and yet that aspect of myself appeared to have gone missing.

Why did it take working with a life coach for me to figure this out? Because I was too involved and invested in all of the other minutiae of my life. I was chest-deep in raising kids, trying to maintain some sort of professional presence in the world, and running a household with now older children who had their own activities and commitments. It had become all-too-easy to forget about my own hopes, dreams, and passions.

It was that life coach who taught me to put myself back on my own list. And once I did, I saw clearly that I hadn't needed to back-burner myself or handbells at all. During that year of traveling back and forth to Lewisburg to play with DP at Bucknell, I proved to myself that indeed the world did not fall apart when I wasn't "Momming." In fact, the kids were better off for it. They got used to babysitters and grew to love them, my husband occasionally had to step up to the plate and figure out "Dadding" without my help, and believe it or not, the house was still standing. No one was suffering from me not being the one to feed or bathe them, no one was claiming I had abandoned them, no one was having nightmares that I was an absent parent.

That year gave me a lot of confidence in being able to pursue what I loved. I realized that when I had been without that outlet, I was less alive, more listless, more melancholy. It wasn't that those feelings had a negative effect on my parenting life or professional life, but when I did make time for handbells and had them in my life on the regular, it made all of the other things that much better. I felt more alive, invigorated, good about using more of my brain, and happy to have an outlet for creativity. You know how people talk about falling in love? How the grass is greener, the sky is bluer, the birds sing more, etc.? Well, to me, that's what having handbells in my life is like.

I hope you are able to enjoy that same feeling. I hope you feel fulfilled with a happy heart and soul that sings for whatever makes you happy. It's true that it might require sacrifice, time, and commitment, but for me, the reward has been greater than any time or effort I've put into my handbell ringing. There has never been a time I have regretted playing handbells (ok, well, maybe on the last concert of a six-concert, two-weekend extravaganza when I had to pack the bells again). But truly, ringing has continually been a blessing. I hope for you that you have at least one thing in your life that provides you the same contentment, peace, and joy.

8

When Following
Our Passions Is Scary

*Music is the greatest form
of communication in the world.*
—Lou Rawls

My heart was racing. I was standing at the back of a hotel breakout room packed with an audience, and I was about to stand in front of them and be a handbell conductor—for the very first time.

The room, which had been so cool and seemed so large over the past four days of the Masterclass in Conducting course I'd taken, now seemed stifling and small. The bells were set up at the front of the room where they'd been all week, but now the area where I and the other students had relaxed and taken breaks was packed with people sitting and standing to listen to our concert. There were well-known composers and conductors, advanced handbell ringers, and other musicians of every level of expertise, but I wasn't supposed to feel any pressure. This, it was explained to me, was a learning experience.

That didn't make me feel any less fearful. My turn to conduct my piece was coming up, and my palms were getting sweatier and sweatier. I wasn't regulating my breathing very well, and my heart was beating out of my chest. I began to think that there was no way I'd make it down that aisle and up on that podium to conduct my piece. I even reasoned that out in my head. In a very matter of fact way, I accepted that I was going to lie down right there at the back of the room and pass out. And that would be okay—I mean, this had been my dream, but someone else would just get up and conduct my piece instead. It would be fine. I resigned myself to the idea I would just pass out, and this would all be over quickly. Certainly no one would expect me to conduct after I'd passed out.

However, with a knot in my throat and feeling completely disassociated from my body, I found myself clapping for the person before me and the piece he'd just conducted. The ringers were mine to lead next. I began walking up that aisle, feeling like my legs would give out at any second. Miraculously, something propelled me forward, and I made it to the podium.

I have no idea what the expression on my face must have been as I faced the crowd. I remember introducing myself with only a slight crack in my voice and bowing to the audience, and then turning around and smiling at my ringers. They gave me comforting smiles back, and I knew that no matter what I did, they would hold it together. That was reassuring.

I know that I made the correct gestures, conducted pretty well, and made good eye contact with them. I managed to remember the entire piece—thank God DP had forced us to memorize each of our pieces despite our protest. I relaxed slightly as the piece went on, and I felt relieved as we approached the end of the song.

I was so happy to conclude the piece that I don't remember cutting off the last chord or having the ringers put their bells down. I know for sure those things happened, and I have the tape to prove it, but I have yet to watch that video. I do remember putting my hand on my heart and mouthing, "Thank you" to them. With that, I turned, bowed, and walked off the podium.

As the next person took her turn at the podium, I felt nothing short of incredulous amazement. I had just done something I was literally scared out of my mind to do—so much so that I'd found it preferable to pass out rather than go through with it. But I did it!

To say I was on an adrenaline high would be a huge understatement. The audience had been generous and kind with their applause, and the few people I knew in the audience even gave some shouts in my honor. That experience of pushing myself to do something scary—and that it was directly related to my passion for music—was exhilarating beyond description. It touched every emotion I had, from complete and utter joy to gratitude, pride, bravery, and relief. In addition to all of that, I did it in front of one of my most admired professors, mentors, and friends. There was nothing more I wanted than to make DP proud, and I felt I did.

The rest of the concert went by in a blur. I was ringing for other conductors just as they had rung for me. They were some of the best ringers I'd ever played with, and what we were able to do in that concert over the space of just four days was nothing short of miraculous. Each of those ringers inspired me to become a better ringer. They raised my level of play.

When it was over, a gratifying number of audience members, including composers and renowned conductors, came up to congratulate us. In fact, that's how I first met esteemed composer Cathy Moklebust. She made sure she complimented every conducting student, and that made a huge impression. So many of these amazing musicians were gracious, reassuring, and encouraging to those of us who had worked so hard to put ourselves up on that podium that day. It reminded me of how strong the musical community is, and how special the connections among handbell ringers are. It gave me such a boost both personally and more globally that humanity truly seeks connection and wants to support each other. What an amazing little nugget to add to the already full experience I had.

I'd always wanted to be a conductor, though I didn't admit that out loud until fairly recently. Ever since I was first exposed to music and learned how to play in a group, my heart has longed to be the leader, the ultimate connector between the music on the page and people playing it. It could be the drive from my Type A personality and German hard-working heritage or a characteristic of being the first born, but whatever it is, it's part of who I am. When I had enough experience to realize the power of making music in a group, I also realized I wanted to be the one to facilitate it, teach it, and encourage the musicians. I want to make other musicians feel the way I do about the power of the music we get to play.

I got to realize part of that dream when I became drum major in high school marching band. I learned much about music and leadership those two years, but I was young and inexperienced, and so were the players I was leading. As my experience and proficiency grew in college, I realized the artistry and true musicality of notes on a page—and that my high school experience hadn't shown me the finesse and beauty of leading a group of really good musicians.

I wanted, it became clear, to conduct handbells.

But I kept the dream to myself. It seemed unattainable, something that might happen in another life, one where I pursued my passions full-time instead of on the side. After all, I would have loved to have majored in music at Bucknell, but I got a Bachelor of Science in Business Administration instead. What extra time I had I gave to Symphonic Band and the Rooke Chapel Ringers, leaving me no time for music electives like conducting. And I feared that since I missed that opportunity in college, it was gone forever.

My dream to conduct probably would have stayed dormant had I not had that opportunity to return to the Rooke Chapel Ringers to ring for DP's last year before retirement. That year renewed my interest in bells. It reminded me how passionate I truly am about this instrument and how much I had missed it being a part of my life. It gave me hope that there was more ringing in my future, and maybe even other opportunities. But life always seem to happen.

It wasn't until a couple years after that, in 2017, that I brought up my dream in a phone call with DP. He and I had a lot of friendly phone conversations, checking on each other, sharing the minutiae of our days.

"I had to take the cats to the vet, and one threw up all over the crate and the car, so now I have to clean the damn car," complained DP.

"I'm so tired of cooking, and I so don't feel like taking the kids to the pool later," I bellyached.

We exchanged stories of which family members were driving us crazy, what errands had to be done, what meetings we each had, and just how much wine would be needed to get through the day.

I remember exactly where I was that morning—outside of our beloved little Italian market in town—when I told him I was bummed I hadn't taken any conducting courses in college and that I wished I had.

"That's not a problem," he said excitedly. "I take private conducting students at the farm all of the time."

Wait, what?

As casually as ever but with such encouragement in his voice, he said, "Ohmygosh, you should totally come to the farm and take the course. I'll send you the information!"

Suddenly, I was going to become a private conducting student of his. To say I was absolutely giddy was an understatement. I knew that if I truly wanted to study conducting, I wanted to learn from the best, and in my book, he is. Since his retirement from Bucknell, he has continued to teach conducting to some of the best bell directors around, both privately and through the aforementioned masterclass at the Handbell Musicians of America National Seminar each year. I had not even known this to be a possibility, and now it could become a reality. I was practically levitating I was so excited.

I was also, typically, thrilled and terrified. In fact, I almost backed out. I remember saying to him on the phone, "Well, you already have my check, so how about you just take that, and I just let this go. I'm willing to forfeit the money. I'm way too nervous!"

The thought of performing in a new way in front of this mentor of mine gave me huge butterflies. Yes, he had been my handbell director and technically professor, but this time I was putting myself out there in a different way, letting myself go back to being a student in a field of study that required lots of demonstration and performance. I was much more comfortable reading from a book and taking a test. I was afraid of embarrassing myself, especially in front of someone I revered so much. I thought it would almost have been easier to learn from a stranger, because given our relationship, I knew we both had expectations of my capabilities. The last thing on the planet I wanted to do was disappoint him or myself. What if I sucked?

Over the course of three days, I studied the equivalent of the first course in conducting, Conducting 101, which is usually taught over a college semester with multiple students. We were in DP's kitchen, a comfortable and welcoming space with dark cherry cabinets, a corner fireplace, and sliding doors leading to a screened-in porch that felt glorious on that early September day. It was difficult not to relax in a setting like that.

We also spent lots of time by the piano in the next room. DP would demonstrate a conducting pattern, and I'd repeat it with my right hand. Then he would add something a little tougher, like doing something else with my left hand, and I'd take a stab at that. Slowly but steadily, we kept increasing the difficulty level of the motions, and I conducted while he played the piano. We worked for four hours that first afternoon, and he gave me homework for the next morning.

We also talked about the role of the conductor and how connection is at the heart of conducting a group. In that moment, my feelings about what I'd always longed for coalesced. No wonder I'd felt such an urge to be a conductor—I'd yearned for human connection my whole life! I'd built strong friendships with people I'd felt strong connections to even when I couldn't explain it. I'd often been the link between someone who needed something and someone who could provide it. Connection has been a common thread in all the areas of my life.

As it turned out, I did pretty well even when I didn't think I was doing so. I found the physical aspect of conducting much more difficult than assimilating the skills a leader needs, like knowing how to facilitate connection and invoking the emotions the music is trying to convey. It was hard and awkward and embarrassing at times, especially for someone with limited hand-eye coordination. And it was intense—lots of information to synthesize in a short amount of time, but it was also fascinating and fabulous.

Forever a student, the rush I got from learning something new, something I had only dreamed of, something I never thought myself capable of, was nothing short of magic. Yes, I had a long way to go, but my smile for accomplishing such a goal was firmly affixed to my face, whether I was alone in the car or sharing my story with someone else. I can recreate that smile just from remembering that time.

Between flute and bells, I was used to performing in a group, not at the front of it. I was scared as hell to do something that put the spotlight on me. Even though leading a group was on my bucket list, I was intimidated—and yet that is exactly where the magic happened. Right there, in my vulnerability, in my fear, in my taking a chance on trying something I've always wanted to do. It was in stretching my passion and reaching for a new level of achievement or accomplishment or simply more enjoyment. It was starting with what I loved and pushing to challenge myself in a new way.

At the conclusion of the private class, the obvious question was what would come next. It's not like you can practice conducting a group without a group to practice with, and no local groups were looking for conductors at the time. But DP was never short of answers. He immediately encouraged me to apply for his Masterclass in Conducting, which takes place right before the HMA's National Seminar each summer.

It would be a great next step, he said excitedly. A chance to work further with him, other conductors, and a group—to really hone my skills and see what I could do. But that would mean submitting an application with an audition video, and I thought that was practically laughable. First of all, I had just gotten started. Second, how was I going to make all of that happen with no group to conduct? I didn't feel I belonged in a room full of more experienced conductors. It even says it in the title: Masterclass.

I had little faith I would be accepted, but I completed my application and was able to submit my videos after the then-director of the Rooke Chapel Ringers allowed me some of his rehearsal time to conduct and record. The ringers were extremely gracious and kind to me as I muddled my way through being recorded.

It was while I was awaiting the decision over the next couple months that I realized how much I wanted to be a part of it, how excited I was at the possibility. How this really, truly was a dream of mine. Then, one morning in mid-April, I woke up to an email that said I had been selected. Woohoo! I was shocked and giddy yet again. And yes, also scared as hell once more. But I knew it was what I was meant to do, because I hadn't been that excited for something in a long time. The thought of taking my passion to the next level, or even simply learning another way to enjoy my passion, was beyond my wildest expectations.

Three short months later, with all of the preparations made (travel arranged, babysitters attained, and music practiced), I left for a week in Michigan. I managed to put off my anxiety while DP and I traveled together to the event, but when the day came to start that Masterclass, I was sure I had bitten off more than I could chew. "What am I doing here?" I thought. "There are people here with loads of experience and I'm simply a novice. They can't possibly be willing to accept me and allow me to learn beside them. I'm an impostor."

I barely ate that first day. I know I was visibly shaky. My mind was going a mile a minute, and I was sure there was a neon flashing sign on my shirt that I couldn't see but others could. "I don't really belong here!" I was sure it said.

As we were waiting to go into the room to begin our class, I considered just skipping out. I looked around at the rest of the students and immediately concluded that everyone was older than me, better than me, more experienced than me, and knew way more than I did. Not a great mindset to start with, but I followed everyone into the room anyway. I was the second person in the line-up of thirteen people who got about thirty-five minutes each to conduct their assigned pieces. Not only were we conducting a group of musicians we'd never met, but the video camera was taping our every move for later study.

All, and I mean all, of this was crazy intimidating to me. The first guy to conduct got up and went through his piece with the ringers while I carefully watched DP's face and gestures for assessment of this dude. I watched how DP interacted with him and gently pointed things out and recommended changes. "Ok, I thought. It doesn't look that bad. Maybe I can pull this off."

When it was my turn, I remember feeling flushed and hoping that thirty-five minutes would just speed by in a blink. And actually, it did. It was uncomfortable at first, for sure, but everyone was kind and gentle. They were very complimentary and told me what they liked about my movements and expressions as I conducted them through my piece, "Coventry Carol," arranged by Brenda Austin, a composer, conductor, and another student in the class.

What I remember most, though, is that each time I got up there, it was like I had one of those digital scrolling boards running through my head the entire time. It would run through all of the techniques I had to use, where I was in the music, and every nuance and tip and adjustment DP made all while I was also trying to concentrate on the quality of the music being played. Every time I got up there, my brain felt like a computer running faster and faster, trying to take in more information and synthesize it in such little time that my head might explode. But each time, just before that happened, my turn would be over as quickly as it had come. It helped that we got a thirty-five minute break after each of our turns conducting to assimilate all of the new information. Phew.

Each day got a little easier, but there were bumps in the road. The second day, emphasis on second as in, the one right after the first, DP surprised each conductor by taking away their music. At first we all laughed, but that only lasted until it was our turn to conduct and he took away our music. He said that we surely had it memorized by this point and that we would get much more musicality out of ourselves and the ringers if we focused solely on that and not the measures in the music, which again, had to be memorized.

It was a struggle at first, but he had a real point, and it made a significant difference in feeling the music and being connected to the ringers with my head out of my music stand. It certainly was another level of nerve-racking to add to the pressure, however.

What made everything so much more bearable were the connections we made. We were in the same room for twelve hours a day for three days, we stayed at the same hotel, we often ate together and grabbed coffee at the same Starbucks. All the while, we were supporting each other, struggling together, laughing together, and making memories together. It's two years later, and the friends I made in that class are just as important to me as they were during that journey.

DP had selected a specific repertoire for us to play and perform, based on the conducting skills he wanted us to learn. The pieces were definitely challenging, and we were all expected to ring at a very high level in a short amount of time. There wasn't a lot of room for error, as we were all trying to do our best for each conductor. DP demanded a lot of us, but we rose to the occasion each time.

As much as I thrive on the connection between the players, the conductor, and the audience, there's something visceral for me in my connection to the notes themselves. I'm one of the lucky people music deeply touches. There are specific notes and chords that can evoke a strong reaction from deep within me.

There are places in Cathy Moklebust's "Resonances and Alleluias" that do just that. It's a beautiful, flowing piece with two contrasting sections: the first a thoughtful but quick-paced minor section, and the second more reflective and melancholy. When the second section resolves into a major-key reprise of the first, I instantly become emotional. I hear a particular chord and immediately feel a lump begin to grow in my throat, my eyes well up with tears. It's involuntary and it happens each and every time, no matter if I'm hearing the piece for the fifth time or the thirty-fifth. I know I am not alone in this phenomenon, and I wish I could explain it scientifically. I also know that other people can garner the same reactions from things that they love. It puzzles and fascinates me each and every time it happens.

Just the other day, my daughter was watching a show on Disney Jr., that uses a lot of classical music. I finally identified what I was hearing (with the help of DP) as Gustav Holtz's "Jupiter" movement from his *The Planets Suite*. It's triumphant and joyous, with a section of reflection that makes me cry every single time I hear it. I have no ties to that particular music otherwise. I simply hear it and invokes a gut reaction that I have trouble putting into words but feel so very deeply. The actual notes and the order they are set in spark a sadness I can't explain. It's different than feeling something during a piece because of the memories it raises. This reaction is completely automatic, uncontrollable, and I would guess, inborn. I feel blessed to have this attachment to music.

At the conclusion of our concert that day in Michigan, even though I had made sure not to make eye contact with him the entire time I was at the podium, DP assured me my next move needed to be conducting a choir. His belief in me was all I wanted to hear, something I've hung onto ever since.

Although that dream hasn't yet been fully realized in the two years since, I've had the chance to substitute conduct for the Rooke Chapel Ringers several times, and I'm putting myself out there as a conductor. I'm planning to continue studying conducting, working with DP, and refining my skills. I know this dream is attainable and out there waiting for me, and when the time is right, it will present itself. In the meantime, I'm learning all I can, taking all of the opportunities to play and conduct that I can, and sharing my story with you.

Whatever your passion is, you can grow it and enjoy it in new ways. Our dreams are out there for us, just waiting for us to grab them.

9

The Magic of It All

Music is the shorthand of emotion.
—Leo Tolstoy

In the 1980s, when I was young, piano lessons for kids were common. At least four or five of my friends were learning piano at the same time I was. My grandmother was an accomplished pianist and organist, and it was assumed I'd love piano too.

I regret that I didn't continue with piano through middle school, but it was an important introduction to music long before music class in school or thoughts of flute, marching band, and especially bells. I'm grateful for where piano lessons eventually led me.

My daughters Ella and Laina have had a much different experience. At an early age, they were introduced to music through classes like Kindermusik. From just a few months old through about age four, I took them to weekly gatherings where we sang songs, played games, experimented with movement, and practiced using our imaginations.

At age nine, Ella took up ukulele because her father was learning guitar. Not long after, she became interested in voice lessons and is now a big fan of Broadway musical theater. We have yet to see what Laina, age eight, might get into musically, but violin, drums, saxophone, and voice lessons have all been thrown around. I'm stalling on the drum set request.

Ella has always taken an interest in my handbell ringing. Laina constantly complains about it. But I know it's made an impact on her because of how vocal she is about it: "I hate bells!" She does, though, have a very sensitive musical ear and has made very mature remarks about all kinds of music. When listening to handbell recordings of my concerts in the car, Laina can pick up on subtleties few other eight-year-olds would. One day, as we were enjoying the very last quiet measures of Matthew Compton's "Spires," a woman in the audience coughed at the absolute worst time. "That lady ruined it," Laina said.

I don't know where Laina's musical talents or interests will lie. But based on her comments about bells and her trying so very hard to hate them, I wouldn't be surprised if she was the one who actually took them up later.

My husband and I would love nothing more for our kids than to have a deep appreciation of music, enjoy all kinds, and create some music of their own. We both have benefitted greatly from music in our lives, both intellectually and emotionally. Beyond the cognitive benefits, on which there is a plethora of research, handbells have taught me about the importance of human connection amidst personal independence. We are our own selves, ringing our own notes—and we need each other to make a pleasing whole.

In order to make beautiful music and what I would call beautiful lives, we need to connect with other humans on a deeper level, feel each other's emotions, even breathe with each other when needed. Humans need emotional ties and support not only to survive but also to thrive, which is what has made the current COVID-19 pandemic especially difficult on top of its already terrifying physical threats.

Humans aren't meant to be separated from each other. We need human conversation, human touch, and the connection that music can give us. Making music together is one of the best bonding experiences there is, and I've felt that most strongly when I ring. It's one of the best things ringing handbells has given me, this reminder that we are all connected.

Handbells has also taught me the importance of communication, since without it, no music can be made. The connection between ringers and that between ringers and conductor allow for the flow of communication that makes truly moving music. The musicians communicating with and connecting to the audience make the difference between an okay performance and a memorable one. And the communication, both verbal and nonverbal, that has to go on between handbell ringers has challenged me and pushed my abilities to communicate clearly. It translates in so many ways to other areas of our lives. After all, we must be clear in what we need and want, in our intentions, and in our responses to each other. That's an important life lesson.

Ringing bells has also reinforced my personal mantra that attention to details make a difference. I have learned that the difference between a good performance and a great performance lies completely in the details, like when notes are damped together, when notes in a chord are rung precisely simultaneously, and how beautiful ringing bells can be visually when everyone rings with the same movements.

There are so many concrete things I've learned from ringing handbells, like rhythms and holding three bells in one hand, and those are all valid. However, the most important things to me have been the more abstract life lessons I've gained from my handbell and conducting experiences. Things I can't begin to put a price on, things that I hope I model for my children as much as possible because they serve all of us so well.

These are also some of the most personal lessons for me. But that doesn't mean they're mine alone. Henri Nouwen, a Dutch Catholic priest, professor, writer, and theologian, coined the phrase, "What's most personal is what's most universal," meaning that often our deepest struggles, our most ethereal joys, and our strongest lessons are also the most common. Your experiences are so similar to mine, and vice versa. We simply have to share them to understand each other.

When I came back to bells in 2013 for a year and then again in 2016, there was an element of fear. Would I remember how to ring? Would it be like riding a bike? Would my age be a detriment now? And most of all, would I disappoint myself or DP or any number of clinicians because I had been one of DP's ringers? That was a lot of weight on my own shoulders, weight I put there myself. In stepping into those nervous spaces, those new situations, I had to allow the fear to become my vulnerability. I had to accept the idea that if I was going to learn new things, I was probably going to screw up along the way, and those mistakes would only make me better. I never in my life felt more vulnerable than I did the day I stood at the back of the Masterclass room awaiting my turn to conduct in public with an audience for the first time.

My beloved grandfather and personal hero used to say, "Put your courage in your back pocket, and take it with you." Well, finding the courage to stand up there that day, in all of my vulnerability, was one of the most singular moments of my life. I felt particularly fragile, inexperienced, and out of my element. But conquering that fear and stepping up on that podium made me feel like I was invincible. The adrenaline rush—and I am not an adrenaline junkie by any stretch—was magical.

Up to that point, I had been very conservative all of my life, particularly with my dreams. I had envisioned a life in which I was a wife and mother and had a successful career in one way or another, but I had never dreamt of conquering any fears or even uncovering dreams I secretly kept to myself, like being a conductor. Even putting that out into the world was a huge step for me.

Keeping myself small didn't do anything for that big dream or for me. And though it was scary as hell—even now, I sometimes think, "Holy crap, how did I do that?"—I learned that I should and will keep doing it. Showing up, trying new things, and pushing myself beyond my comfort zone is the exact place where the magic happens.

To me, it feels like standing on a cliff, on the edge of possibility, deciding whether or not to jump even though I know I can fly. And then taking that leap—and soaring. There's nothing like it, and music has taught me that again and again. I'm so grateful for pushing through my vulnerability and fear and finding my courage because it has led to extraordinary experiences I could never have imagined.

For me, passion creates possibility. Finding that passion, making room for it in my life, and sticking to it have made me realize that in order to reach those soaring moments, I must also be authentically myself. I can't hold back. I can't hide the parts of me that I think others might not accept. I have to fully step into myself, make the choices that are authentically mine, and be loyal to my own instincts and no one else's. I can feel afraid, I can be nervous, and I can be uncomfortable, but there's a difference between feeling those emotions due to growth and feeling those emotions due to a bad situation.

If I feel those emotions in an excited way when I'm working on pursuing a goal, I know I am on the right path. It feels right, aligned with what's in my heart and my head. If I try to do something that's not really authentically me, I won't feel those good things.

Sometimes that happens to all of us, and we push ahead anyway because someone else is pressuring us or we're afraid we'll disappoint them. But then we feel awful. Those awful feelings tell us we're not being authentically ourselves, and what we're aiming for may not be on our true path. In other words, not everyone is a handbell enthusiast.

I could have easily chosen not to play handbells in college. They're pretty, but they're quirky. I could have decided they were too weird and gone for something more mainstream (and more economical) to play. But I like things that are a little uncommon, the things that not everyone loves. Those bells were and are authentically me, and I will talk about them to anyone anytime until I'm blue in the face because I love them so much. Through and through, I'm a bell geek.

Handbells have also reminded me, time and time again, that humility is a virtuous characteristic to live by. It's so much fun when music comes together and performances are almost flawless and the energy of the audience and the ringers play off of each other. It's a great confidence boost when I've learned a new bell skill and get to show it off. It's an ego boost when my neighbor and I have mastered a passage and are asked to demonstrate it for the group.

Then there are the times when things fall apart: when the concert completely sucks, or someone drops a bell on the floor to a loud crack, or the conductor forgets which piece is next. I've had so many of those awful, embarrassing moments. One happened just a year and a half ago when I was playing with the Rooke Chapel Ringers at a festival in State College, Pennsylvania, where DP was the clinician. I felt pretty good about myself because I was filling in for the RCR at the last minute and sight reading some music on the same day we were going to give a concert. I was pretty confident and excited. That was, until I was the one who knocked a bell onto the gym floor.

I tried to be as calm as possible, but I know my face was fire engine red. I was so embarrassed because of course these were not my bells. I didn't even look up to see the expression on DP's face. I wanted to crawl under the table for the rest of the afternoon. But alas, I had to keep ringing and just hope that people forgot about that. When I later sarcastically asked DP how he liked my gaffe, he replied, "Yeah, I tried to ignore that." D'oh.

There was another time about a year ago when I was playing with the Hershey Handbell Ensemble, a community group, throughout the concert season. I believe it was the second concert of our series, and I was having a really great night. I was greatly pleased with my playing and was really feeling in the groove. As our conductor was introducing the next piece, we got in our places and put our hands on our bells. I put my bells up as everyone else did, and several of us shared the first note. Except when I rang mine, it was not the right note. It was a sharp/flat when it should have been a natural. It stuck out so much that we actually started laughing and had to start again.

Somehow, the person previously on my position had left two of the same bell on the table while the bell I needed was underneath the table. This had never happened before, but apparently this time he forgot to switch the bells back after he needed them that way for his part in the previous song. Damn. Big mistake. Probably one for the books, but hey, we all make them. It keeps us honest. It keeps us humble.

Humility doesn't just mean shrugging off mistakes or keeping your ego in check. It also means having the courage to ask for help when you need it. Handbell music can get very difficult, and that's why each piece is assigned a level. When ringing a level 4, 5, or 6 piece, things can get very intricate and tricky. They use more bells and oftentimes handchimes as well. There may not be enough hands to cover all of the bells in each part. A lot of problem- and puzzle-solving goes on.

One of the most important things that successful ringers and groups as a whole do is reach out to another ringer for help. Asking for help is not a weakness but an admittance that the music would sound better if someone else covered a particular note in a passage. Sometimes that means giving a bell to our next-door neighbor, and other times it means giving a bell to someone five or six people down the line. Sometimes it means finding an extra bell and doubling a part or asking someone who has a quieter part to cover more action.

I've never been good at asking for help. I was raised to be independent and able to do whatever I need to do for myself. In this day and age, being a mom is a particularly challenging role because the media, the role models, and all of the examples that are set for us show supermoms who can do it all. Moms share Pinterest ideas for everything from birthday parties to boxed lunches, and most moms' Facebook pages are filled with the highlights, not the drudgery of the everyday. Therefore, it's become very ingrained that we shouldn't need help.

Playing in handbell choirs has helped me practice asking for assistance. When I can't master something and the music is going to suffer for it, the best thing to do is ask for someone to help. Everyone is better off for it, and the music improves tremendously. It may not always be easy to ask for help, but that lesson in humility is a reminder.

10

When Your Passion Sneaks Up on You

We shall not cease from exploration
And the end of our exploring
Will be to arrive where we started
And know the place for the first time.
–T.S. Elliot

That Sunday morning in the Rooke Chapel, the college freshman version of me had no idea that the goosebumps rising on her arms were the beginning of a rewarding, lifelong relationship with handbells. I feel great affection for her and no small amount of pride. She didn't let a negative experience keep her from connecting to something that moved her anew. She showed determination when it would have been so, so much easier to quit. She went all-in on what, after all, was a rather unlikely passion. When ringing came back into her life, she said yes—even though, not so long before, she'd told it very firmly to go away.

I'm a little envious of her too. Her entire life was before her, and she had no idea what was about to unfold. She didn't know that ringing and building relationships in the handbell community would bring her untold joy, connection, and adventure. She, homesick, anxious, mildly depressed, couldn't have imagined how much good was going to come her way just because of the shiny piece of bronze she was about to put in her hand. She had yet to discover that handbells would make all of the threads in her life make sense, a home she'd come back to again and again.

And that's how it is. Our passions don't always announce themselves loudly or make a grand entrance. Sometimes they come knocking loudly at the front door. Sometimes they tiptoe in silently in the still of night. They might be old friends (or nemeses) circling back to present themselves once again, like handbells were for me, or they might be surprising strangers. The secret to recognizing them is to keep an open mind and an open heart. To pay attention to what piques our interest. To honor the goosebumps.

We are all so beautifully different, and so are the things that light us up. Whatever our passion may be, we will know it by the way it ignites our spirits and inspires us to nurture it from deep within our souls. Our passion is more than a hobby; it's part of our purpose. It is the thing that proclaims that we aren't just living, but that we are fully alive.

Epilogue

When I completed this book (or thought I did), I knew my handbell story wasn't over. But I had no idea of the incredible surprise in store for me just a few days later.

A week after this book launched on Kindle, I turned 42. Not a milestone birthday, so I certainly wasn't expecting a milestone gift. I got some workout weights and some puzzles, both welcome pandemic gifts. Friends sent flowers and gift cards. I felt loved.

For a couple weeks leading up to that day, my husband, Fred, had been repeatedly asking me what my plans were. I had reminded him of the ongoing pandemic. "Dude, I have exactly nothing going on. We can't go anywhere, we can't do anything, so yeah, nothing."

"Well, I might have something planned for the morning," he'd said. "We might have to be here."

I didn't think much about it at first. But as the days passed, the sketchier—and more intriguing—his story became. When I pressed him, he told me, "Someone wants to wish you a happy birthday. I didn't even know that you knew this person."

Now I getting a little nervous. What did he mean? Who was he talking about? "This better not be some weird singing telegram or something," I warned him.

"Well, it might be kind of weird," Fred said, "so just keep that in mind."

At that point, I wanted him to give up the surprise. He wouldn't.

I was on the phone with a friend from Texas on the morning of my birthday when I saw a white Honda CRV pull up to our house and back into our driveway. There was an older couple in the driver and passenger seats, and the license plates were from North Carolina. I had no idea who these people were. I was up for a surprise, but I wasn't up for strange. I was a little worried.

Without a word to me, Fred masked up and walked out to greet the couple as they got out of their car. Not knowing what else to do, I hung up the phone and put on my own mask. As I was grabbing my coat, I glanced out to the driveway and saw that the back of the car was open. The trunk was filled with handbell cases, tables, and padding.

Standing alone in the kitchen for a split second, I said aloud, "Oh my God. Oh my God." There was a part of me wondering—well, hoping—it was going to be mine.

I walked out of our garage. The woman, slender, silver-haired, and tiny, held three handbells. Fred had his phone out and started recording as the woman, who we'll call Mrs. M., began to sing and ring me "Happy Birthday." It was lovely and sweet, and she was so excited to celebrate with me.

As she finished, I thought, "Oh, how nice was that. It must have been a singing telegram type thing. It was nice of everyone to go to that trouble." I assumed that was the end of the surprise, and my heart sank just a little.

Mrs. M. wished me a happy birthday, and we began to chat. I have no idea what we talked about because at some point she said, "All of this is yours," and my brain locked up. I'm pretty sure I said, "What?" at least two or three times, but only Fred's recording knows. My jaw dropped behind my mask. I felt like I was having an out-of-body experience. Maybe I was dreaming? I had no idea what to say.

When I finally got my bearings, Mrs. M. and her husband explained to me that everything in the trunk, which had belonged to her for many years, was now mine: three octaves of Schulmerich bells, five Perry bell tables, and everything that came along with them.

Still feeling shocked, I helped them unload everything and take it into our living room. It had been over a year since I'd hauled a bell case or table, and picking the first one up and reminding myself what it was like to carry that weight felt amazing. The sensation was almost electric, like a current of excitement running from the case up my arm and through my body. I could *not* believe this was happening.

Mrs. M. proudly showed me everything, from the polished bells to the tables, the built-in music stands, and every little extra that was neatly tucked in each bell case—gloves, polish, polishing cloths, literature, a tool set, and more. In a few minutes' time, I'd gone from only being able to touch a bell at church or an event to having my own living room prepped for a small choir. It was surreal.

We inspected every piece of equipment, chatted about our families, and prayed together over the bells. I thanked Mr. and Mrs. M. profusely for at least the fifteenth time, and we said goodbye and sent them on their way.

I stood in my living room, still shocked at what had transpired, and tried to wrap my head around the idea that what I love so much, the passion I dream about and had just written about, the things I most love to make music with, were right there in front of me. I had to stand back for a minute and just gawk at the shiny bronze on the black cloth. There were so many bells and tables that they ran from the front of the living into our family room at the back of the house.

I turned to my husband in amazement. I know I asked him at least twice, "Are these really mine?" Both times he reassured me they were, and then I asked the million-dollar question: How? How did he do this?

Fred told me the sweetest, most hilarious, and most romantic story a bell geek could ever imagine. He'd been wanting to buy me bells for a long time, but he couldn't find any sets for sale. Finally, he started coming across some options online, but he needed some professional expertise, so he called DP.

Of course DP was part of this. How could he not be?

At first, Fred found a small set of Malmark bells. He consulted DP, and DP lovingly said, "No, she's going to want Schulmerichs." Truth.

Then Fred found a two-octave set of Schulmerichs and called DP back. "I'm pretty sure she's going to want three octaves," DP said.

Fred must have thought DP was busting his budget, but he went back to the internet a third time and found Mrs. M.'s handbells for sale through her ad on the Handbell Musicians of America website. She was asking slightly more than he wanted to pay, but he made an offer anyway. She told him she was waiting on one other offer, and she would get back to him.

Luckily for us, the other person who made an offer didn't want the included tables, only the bells, and she wanted everything as a package. Fred wanted all of it. She came back to Fred and told him she'd accept his offer and that she and her husband were planning a trip to our area in April to visit family, so they could deliver the bells directly to us.

Fred was thrilled and relieved. He told Mrs. M. that he would print a photo of the bells to give me on my birthday and tell me they were coming in April.

But handbells, as I know by now, have their own kind of magic. A day or two later, Mrs. M. called Fred again. She and her husband had called their family in Pennsylvania to see if they could change their trip to February—in time for my birthday. Their family agreed, so they intended to leave North Carolina within a day or two, spend time with family, and then deliver my bells to our door right on my birthday.

Fred couldn't believe it. Mrs. M. said she and her husband loved the story of how Fred wanted to surprise me on my birthday so much that they couldn't miss the opportunity to surprise me on my actual birthday. Now all Fred had to do was figure out how to keep quiet until the big day arrived.

So there Fred and I were, on my birthday, in my living room, staring incredulously at these bells that were seemingly everywhere. I kept peppering Fred with questions—when did this happen, who knew the secret, how did he pay for these, was DP in on it the whole time?

Over the course of the past couple of weeks, I've gotten my answers, and the funniest things have come from these new additions to our living room. Ella had been in on the secret and kept it like a champ, but the bells were a total surprise to Laina, the one who hated bells the most. The morning after they came, she came running downstairs and wanted to grab all of them at once, ringing them as loudly as possible.

I said, "Hey Laina, I thought you hated bells."

She replied, "Well, that's because I didn't have any before. Now I have my own to play!" Although I remind her they aren't actually *her* bells, I love her enthusiasm and change of heart. Bell magic.

But the most hilarious thing to come out of the entire experience was and remains a quick text exchange Fred had with my brother-in-law. "I just sold my bass clarinet so I could buy my wife handbells," Fred texted.

My brother-in-law texted back. "Dude, that's the nerdiest sentence I've ever read in my entire life."

That would be true. But for this handbell geek, married to a saxophone and clarinet geek, it's one of the best, most romantic things ever. And as I'm watching Fred and the girls interact with the bells, I'm aware, more than ever, of how much possibility there is in the passions that move us.

"We should start a family choir!" says Laina.

Acknowledgments

This book would have not been possible without the steadfast support and leadership of my editors, Maggie McReynolds and Sky Kier. In fact, this book would not have come to fruition at all if it hadn't been for Maggie's insight and encouragement to write about my passion, something that lights me up from the inside out. We didn't quite know what this book was going to look like when we started, in the midst of a pandemic no less, and there is no roadmap when you don't know where you're going. However, even when I wanted to give up, your support never wavered. I can't thank you both enough for your reassurance, confidence in me, and facilitation of my growth as a writer through this book. It was a true labor of love, an emotional journey, and a process I will be forever grateful that we went through together.

Thank you to those who have brought music into my life, as without them, there would be no story to write. My love of music began with my grandmother, Nancy Zimmerman, who taught me to play the piano. Numerous music and band teachers in middle school and high school set a firm foundation for my growing appreciation of the art. To my flute teachers Cristal Sheaffer and Mary Hannigan, you raised my level of play and inspired me every time we were together. To Dr. William Kenny at Bucknell University, you showed me what musicians can truly do with notes on a page. I had no idea what we were capable of doing, and for your direction, I am grateful.

Without all of you, I would not have come to love the craft and would not have come to handbells.

My most sincere thank you and love to Dr. William Payn, the man who changed music for me forever. Not only is simply being in your presence an inspiration, but being able to make music for and with you will always be a blessing and privilege of my life. Thank you, DP, for your leadership, your knowledge, your desire to connect, and your willingness to take a chance on me. I had no idea when I walked into that chapel to audition for the Rooke Chapel Ringers that it would change the trajectory of my life in such a profound way. Thank you for always being there for me, personally and professionally, and always telling me how capable I am. Thank you for being such a good sport about this book and some of the little, inside jokes I revealed. Thank you to both you and Ruth for your never-ending support, encouragement, and unconditional love.

Thank you to my husband Fred, and my two beautiful girls who are now getting used to Mom spending time writing. I had originally planned to write the bulk of this book before the kids finished school in the spring of 2020 so we could spend a lot of the summer together, but the COVID-19 pandemic had other plans. So, I thank all three of you for your patience, the time you gave me to write, and the interest you take in my work. Girls, I hope the love and appreciation that Daddy and I have for music will rub off on the both of you.

Thank you to the family and friends who have encouraged me through this second and more difficult journey to produce a book. Thank you to Lisa, my life coach and forever friend and cheerleader. I love you huge. Thank you to my fellow Un-Settling Books authors. I can't wait until this pandemic is over and we can be together again. Thank you to my closest supporters, Jen, Mary, Pam, and Sara. You never stopped reassuring me of who I am and what I can do, even when I wanted to quit. I hope you get to learn the depth of my passion through this book. I love you.

Finally, thank you to those who contributed to this book, especially those in the handbell world. Brian Childers, Cathy Moklebust, Jenny Cauhorn, and Dave Harris, I can't tell you how much I appreciate your willingness to talk about this passion we have for ringing. Thank you for your knowledge and perspective. And a massive thank you to all of the former Rooke Chapel Ringers I called upon for memories from good and crazy times. What we share as RCR alumni is unlike anything else in my life.

Resources

Websites

Brian Childers
    brianchilders.org
Cathy Moklebust
    cathymoklebust.com
David Harris and The Raleigh Ringers
    rr.org
Handbell Musicians of America
    handbellmusicians.org
Malmark Bellcraftsmen
    malmark.com
Melmark Pennslvania
    melmark.org
Ringing Cavaliers, Veterans Bridge to Recovery Program,
Minneapolis VA Health Care System
    minneapolis.va.gov/services/VBR.asp
Rooke Chapel Ringers of Bucknell University
    bucknell.edu/academics/college-arts-sciences/
    academic-departments-programs/music/ensembles/
    rooke-chapel-ringers
Schulermich
    schulmerichbells.com
Dr. William Payn, Conductor
    svcmusic.org/about/conductor/

Books

Childers, Brian. *Ringing Deeply: A devotional book for handbell ringers, directors, and fans.* 2018.

About the Author

Hillary Marotta has been a musician almost all of her life. She began learning to play the piano at age six, followed quickly by the flute. Though she only took several years of piano, she has played flute through all of her school years, college, and beyond in community bands and church settings. She began ringing handbells in sixth grade but took a long  hiatus until she heard handbells at Bucknell University. She spent three years as a Rooke Chapel Ringer under Dr. William Payn's direction and has reprised her role several times since on multiple occasions for varying lengths of time. Hillary has also rung for church groups in Virginia and Pennsylvania as well as the Hershey Handbell Ensemble. She was selected to play in two Distinctly Bronze audition-only events through the Handbell Musicians of America organization. In addition, Hillary has studied conducting under Dr. William Payn's baton and served as a substitute conductor for the Rooke Chapel Ringers on multiple occasions. Hillary hopes to conduct her own handbell group in the future.

Hillary is also a nonprofit specialist, a Mental Health First Aid Trainer, and a mother of two. She is the author of *Head and Heart: How to Run a Smart & Compassionate Nonprofit* and consults with several nonprofits in Central Pennsylvania. She has served as a guest speaker and lecturer on nonprofits at her alma mater, Bucknell University. She is also heavily involved in many nonprofit organizations and her church. She and her husband live with their two girls, their handsome goldendoodle Teddy, and standoff-ish cat Morris in Hummelstown, PA. She enjoys reading, writing, spending time with friends, and traveling. If she could live year-round in a tropical paradise, she would. You can find Hillary at hillarymarotta.com and on Facebook at Hillary Marotta Author, where she'd love to share more with you.

Made in the USA
Monee, IL
20 December 2022

23017076R00098